# Image-Based Modeling
# of Plants and Trees

# Synthesis Lectures on Computer Vision

Editors
**Gérard Medioni,** *University of Southern California*
**Sven Dickinson,** *University of Toronto*

**Image-Based Modeling of Plants and Trees**
Sing Bing Kang and Long Quan
2009

Image-Based Modeling of Plants and Trees

Sing Bing Kang and Long Quan

ISBN: 978-3-031-00680-7      paperback

ISBN: 978-3-031-01808-4      ebook

DOI 10.1007/978-3-031-01808-4

A Publication in the Springer series

*SYNTHESIS LECTURES ON ADVANCES IN AUTOMOTIVE TECHNOLOGY*

Lecture #1

Series Editors: Gérard Medioni, *University of Southern California*

                        Sven Dickinson, *University of Toronto*

Series ISSN

Synthesis Lectures on Computer Vision

ISSN pending.

# Image-Based Modeling of Plants and Trees

Sing Bing Kang
Microsoft Research

Long Quan
The Hong Kong University of Science and Technology

*SYNTHESIS LECTURES ON COMPUTER VISION #1*

# ABSTRACT

Plants and trees are among the most complex natural objects. Much work has been done attempting to model them, with varying degrees of success. In this book, we review the various approaches in computer graphics, which we categorize as rule-based, image-based, and sketch-based methods.

We describe our approaches for modeling plants and trees using images. Image-based approaches have the distinct advantage that the resulting model inherits the realistic shape and complexity of a real plant or tree. We use different techniques for modeling plants (with relatively large leaves) and trees (with relatively small leaves). With plants, we model each leaf from images, while for trees, the leaves are only approximated due to their small size and large number. Both techniques start with the same initial step of structure from motion on multiple images of the plant or tree that is to be modeled.

For our plant modeling system, because we need to model the individual leaves, these leaves need to be segmented out from the images. We designed our plant modeling system to be interactive, automating the process of shape recovery while relying on the user to provide simple hints on segmentation. Segmentation is performed in both image and 3D spaces, allowing the user to easily visualize its effect immediately. Using the segmented image and 3D data, the geometry of each leaf is then automatically recovered from the multiple views by fitting a deformable leaf model. Our system also allows the user to easily reconstruct branches in a similar manner.

To model trees, because of the large leaf count, small image footprint, and widespread occlusions, we do not model the leaves exactly as we do for plants. Instead, we populate the tree with leaf replicas from segmented source images to reconstruct the overall tree shape. In addition, we use the shape patterns of visible branches to predict those of obscured branches. As a result, we are able to design our tree modeling system so as to minimize user intervention.

We also handle the special case of modeling a tree from only a single image. Here, the user is required to draw strokes on the image to indicate the tree crown (so that the leaf region is approximately known) and to refine the recovery of branches. As before, we concatenate the shape patterns from a library to generate the 3D shape.

To substantiate the effectiveness of our systems, we show realistic reconstructions of a variety of plants and trees from images. Finally, we offer our thoughts on improving our systems and on the remaining challenges associated with plant and tree modeling.

## KEYWORDS

tree modeling, plant modeling, image-based modeling

# Contents

Figure Credits . . . . . . . . . . . . . . . . . . . . . . . . . . . . . . . . . . . . . . . . . . . . . . . . . . . . . . . . ix

1   Introduction . . . . . . . . . . . . . . . . . . . . . . . . . . . . . . . . . . . . . . . . . . . . . . . . . . . . . . . 1

2   Review of Plant and Tree Modeling Techniques . . . . . . . . . . . . . . . . . . . . . . . . . . . . . 5

    2.1  Rule-based methods . . . . . . . . . . . . . . . . . . . . . . . . . . . . . . . . . . . . . . . . . . . . 5

    2.2  Sketch-based methods . . . . . . . . . . . . . . . . . . . . . . . . . . . . . . . . . . . . . . . . . . 9

    2.3  Image-based methods . . . . . . . . . . . . . . . . . . . . . . . . . . . . . . . . . . . . . . . . . . 11

    2.4  Modeling Leaves, Flowers, and Bark . . . . . . . . . . . . . . . . . . . . . . . . . . . . . . 13

    2.5  Modeling Environmental Effects . . . . . . . . . . . . . . . . . . . . . . . . . . . . . . . . . 15

    2.6  Modeling Other Flora . . . . . . . . . . . . . . . . . . . . . . . . . . . . . . . . . . . . . . . . . 16

    2.7  Appendix: Brief description of L-system . . . . . . . . . . . . . . . . . . . . . . . . . . . 16

3   Image-Based Technique for Modeling Plants . . . . . . . . . . . . . . . . . . . . . . . . . . . . . . 19

    3.1  Overview of Plant Modeling System . . . . . . . . . . . . . . . . . . . . . . . . . . . . . . 19

    3.2  Preliminary Processes . . . . . . . . . . . . . . . . . . . . . . . . . . . . . . . . . . . . . . . . . 19

    3.3  Graph-based Leaf Extraction . . . . . . . . . . . . . . . . . . . . . . . . . . . . . . . . . . . 20

         3.3.1  Graph partition    21

         3.3.2  User interface    23

         3.3.3  Graph update    23

         3.3.4  Boundary segmentation    24

    3.4  Model-based Leaf Reconstruction . . . . . . . . . . . . . . . . . . . . . . . . . . . . . . . . 24

         3.4.1  Extraction of a generic leaf model    24

         3.4.2  Leaf reconstruction    24

    3.5  Branch Extraction and Reconstruction . . . . . . . . . . . . . . . . . . . . . . . . . . . . 26

    3.6  Results . . . . . . . . . . . . . . . . . . . . . . . . . . . . . . . . . . . . . . . . . . . . . . . . . . . . 27

    3.7  Discussion . . . . . . . . . . . . . . . . . . . . . . . . . . . . . . . . . . . . . . . . . . . . . . . . . . 31

3.8     Summary . . . . . . . . . . . . . . . . . . . . . . . . . . . . . . . . . . . . . . . . . . . . . . . . . . . . . 32

4     Image-Based Technique for Modeling Trees . . . . . . . . . . . . . . . . . . . . . . . . . . . . . . . 33

4.1     Overview of the system . . . . . . . . . . . . . . . . . . . . . . . . . . . . . . . . . . . . . . . . . . 33

4.2     Image capture and 3D point recovery . . . . . . . . . . . . . . . . . . . . . . . . . . . . . . . . 35

4.3     Branch recovery . . . . . . . . . . . . . . . . . . . . . . . . . . . . . . . . . . . . . . . . . . . . . . . . . 35

      4.3.1   Reconstruction of visible branches     35

      4.3.2   Reconstruction of occluded branches     37

4.4     Populating the tree with leaves . . . . . . . . . . . . . . . . . . . . . . . . . . . . . . . . . . . . 39

      4.4.1   Image segmentation and clustering     39

      4.4.2   Adding leaves to branches     41

4.5     Results . . . . . . . . . . . . . . . . . . . . . . . . . . . . . . . . . . . . . . . . . . . . . . . . . . . . . . . 42

4.6     Discussion . . . . . . . . . . . . . . . . . . . . . . . . . . . . . . . . . . . . . . . . . . . . . . . . . . . . . 45

4.7     Summary . . . . . . . . . . . . . . . . . . . . . . . . . . . . . . . . . . . . . . . . . . . . . . . . . . . . . . 45

5     Single Image Tree Modeling . . . . . . . . . . . . . . . . . . . . . . . . . . . . . . . . . . . . . . . . . . . 49

5.1     Overview of System . . . . . . . . . . . . . . . . . . . . . . . . . . . . . . . . . . . . . . . . . . . . . 49

5.2     Image Plane Sketching . . . . . . . . . . . . . . . . . . . . . . . . . . . . . . . . . . . . . . . . . . . 49

5.3     Tree Growing . . . . . . . . . . . . . . . . . . . . . . . . . . . . . . . . . . . . . . . . . . . . . . . . . . . 53

      5.3.1   Growth engine     54

      5.3.2   Data-driven attractors     56

5.4     Completing the Tree . . . . . . . . . . . . . . . . . . . . . . . . . . . . . . . . . . . . . . . . . . . . . 57

5.5     Results . . . . . . . . . . . . . . . . . . . . . . . . . . . . . . . . . . . . . . . . . . . . . . . . . . . . . . . 57

5.6     Summary . . . . . . . . . . . . . . . . . . . . . . . . . . . . . . . . . . . . . . . . . . . . . . . . . . . . . . 62

6     Summary and Concluding Remarks . . . . . . . . . . . . . . . . . . . . . . . . . . . . . . . . . . . . 63

7     Acknowledgments . . . . . . . . . . . . . . . . . . . . . . . . . . . . . . . . . . . . . . . . . . . . . . . . . . . 65

Bibliography . . . . . . . . . . . . . . . . . . . . . . . . . . . . . . . . . . . . . . . . . . . . . . . . . . . . . . . . . . 67

Authors' Biographies . . . . . . . . . . . . . . . . . . . . . . . . . . . . . . . . . . . . . . . . . . . . . . . . . . 73

# Figure Credits

**Figure 2.1** is from

P. Prusinkiewicz, M. Hammel, J. Hanan, and R. Mech, "L-systems: from the theory to visual models of plants," In M. T. Michalewicz (Ed.), Proceedings of the 2nd CSIRO Symposium on Computational Challenges in Life Sciences. CSIRO Publishing, 1996. Reprinted by permission.

**Figure 2.2** is from

P. de Reffye, C. Edelin, J. Francon, M. Jaeger, and C. Puech, "Plant models faithful to botanical structure and development," ACM SIGGRAPH, pp. 151-158, 1988, ©1988 Association for Computing Machinery, Inc. Reprinted by permission.

http://doi.acm.org/10.1145/54852.378505.

**Figure 2.3** is from

J. Weber and J. Penn, "Creation and rendering of realistic trees," ACM SIGGRAPH, pp. 119-127, 1995. ©1995 Association for Computing Machinery, Inc. Reprinted by permission.

http://doi.acm.org/10.1145/218380.218427.

**Figure 2.4** is from

B. Lintermann and O. Deussen, "Interactive modeling of plants," IEEE Computer Graphics and Applications," 19(1):56-65, 1999. Copyright ©1999 IEEE. Reprinted by permission.

http://doi.ieeecomputersociety.org/10.1109/38.736469.

**Figure 2.5** is from

Makoto Okabe, Shigeru Owada, Takeo Igarashi, "Interactive Design of Botanical Trees Using Free-hand Sketches and Example-based Editing", Computer Graphics Forum (Proc. Eurographics 2005), Volume 24, Issue 3, pp. 487-496, Eurographics 2005, copyright ©2005, Wiley Blackwell. Reprinted by permission.

http://dx.doi.org/10.1111/j.1467-8659.2005.00874.x.

**Figure 2.6** is from

X. Chen, B. Neubert, Y.-Q. Xu, O. Deussen, and S.B. Kang, "Sketch-based tree modeling using Markov random field," *ACM SIGGRAPH Asia and ACM Transaction on Graphics*, 27(5), article 109, 2008. ©2008 Association for Computing Machinery, Inc. Reprinted by permission.

http://doi.acm.org/10.1145/1457515.1409062.

**Figure 2.7** is from

Reche-Martinez, I. Martin, and G. Drettakis, "Volumetric reconstruction and interactive rendering of trees from photographs," ACM SIGGRAPH, 23(3):720-727, 2004. ©2004 Association for Computing Machinery, Inc. Reprinted by permission.

http://doi.acm.org/10.1145/1015706.1015785.

**Figure 2.8** is from
B. Neubert, T. Franken, and O. Deussen, "Approximate image-based tree-modelling using particle flows," ACM SIGGRAPH, 26(3), article 88, 2007. ©2007 Association for Computing Machinery, Inc. Reprinted by permission.
http://doi.acm.org/10.1145/1275808.1276487.

# CHAPTER 1

# Introduction

Plants and trees remain the most difficult kinds of object to model due to their complex geometry and wide variation in appearance.

**Figure 1.1:** Plants and trees come in all shapes and sizes.

While significant progress has been made over the years in modeling plants and trees, ease of model generation, model editability, and realism are difficult to achieve simultaneously. Once the realistic geometry of a plant or tree has been extracted, it can be used in a number of ways, for example, as part of an architectural design or realistic-looking environments for movie post-production, in games or web applications, or even for the scientific study of plant growth. By predicting plant and tree growth, the look and maintenance of cities can be reasonably planned ahead of time. Furthermore, if geometry is available, the tree model can be easily manipulated or edited.

As we shall see in the next chapter, the techniques for generating plant and tree models are highly varied. While techniques have been proposed to synthetically generate realistic-looking plants, they either require expertise to use (e.g., Prusinkiewicz et al. (1994)), or they are highly manually intensive. Sketch-based techniques are getting more sophisticated, and more practical; systems such as that of Chen et al. (2008) require only a simple drawing of a tree to generate realistic-looking models. Image-based techniques that use images of real plants have either produced models that are not easily manipulated (e.g., Reche-Martinez et al. (2004)) or models that are just approximations (e.g., Shlyakhter et al. (2001)).

The techniques described in Chapters 3 and 4 are image-based as well, but we explicitly extract geometry, and we strictly enforce geometric compatibility across the input images. Image acquisition is simple: the camera need not be calibrated, and the images can be freely taken around the plant of interest. Our modeling system is designed to take advantage of the robust structure from motion algorithm developed in the computer vision community. It is also designed to allow the user to quickly recover the remaining details in the form of individual leaves and branches. Furthermore, it does not require any expertise in botany to use. We show how plants with complicated geometry can be constructed with relative ease. One of the motivations for developing an image-based approach to plant modeling is that the geometry computation from images tends to work remarkably well for textured objects (Hartley and Zisserman (2000)), and the plants are often well-textured. In Chapter 5, we deal with the constraint that only *one* image of the tree is available.

We have a preference for image-based approaches because we believe such approaches have the best potential for producing realistic tree models. The capture process is simple as it involves only a hand-held camera. We use a structure from motion technique to recover the camera motion and 3D point cloud of the plant or tree from a set of images with significant baselines. More specifically, we use the approach described in Lhuillier and Quan (2005) to compute a quasi-dense cloud of reliable 3D points in space. This technique was selected because it provides reasonably robust and accurate reconstruction results for widely separated images. Dense stereo techniques such as those of Goesele et al. (2007) and Tola et al. (2008) may also be used.

In the case of plant modeling (Chapter 3), the system assists in segmenting leaves and extracting their 3D shape. It also assists the user in adding branches. In the case of tree modeling (Chapter 4), rather than applying specific rules for branch generation, we use the local shapes of branches that are observed to interpolate those of obscured branches. The small leaves are generated by segmenting the source images and computing their depths using the pre-computed 3D points or based on proximity to the recovered branches. In each case, design decisions were made to minimize user interaction given what computer vision algorithms can reliably offer.

In Chapter 5, which handles the case of tree modeling from a single image, we require the user to draw strokes to allow the system to segment out leaves and branches more effectively. Because only one image is available, structure from motion cannot be used. Instead, we use a library of 3D branch shapes to construct the tree model such that its projection closely approximates the segmented 2D branches.

Note that in this book, we differentiate between plants and trees—we consider "plants" as terrestrial flora with large discernible leaves (relative to the plant size), and "trees" as large terrestrial flora with small leaves (relative to the tree size). The spectrum of plants and trees with varying leaf sizes is shown in Figure 1.2. This book does not cover modeling of tree details; techniques for generating realistic models of flowers (Ijiri et al. (2005)), bark (Lefebvre and Neyret (2002); Wang et al. (2003)), and leaves (Wang et al. (2005)) are covered elsewhere.

Plants with large
discernible leaves

Trees with small
undiscernible leaves

**Figure 1.2:** Spectrum of plants and trees based on relative leaf size: on the left end of the spectrum, the size of the leaves relative to the plant is large. This is ideal for using the modeling system described in Chapter 3. The modeling system described in Chapter 4, on the other hand, targets trees with small relative leaf sizes (compared to the entire tree).

# CHAPTER 2

# Review of Plant and Tree Modeling Techniques

Techniques for computer-generated plants and trees were introduced as early as 1966 by Ulam (1966). Since then, a variety of techniques have been proposed to model and generate plants and trees; they can be roughly classified as primarily being rule-based, sketch-based, or image-based. Note that these classes of techniques are not mutually exclusive (e.g., a technique can be sketch-based but uses production rules for the final model generation).

In this chapter, we give a brief review of the techniques used for modeling plants and trees. Our review is not meant to be exhaustive; more detailed expositions on tree modeling can be found in texts such as Prusinkiewicz and Lindenmayer (1990) and Deussen and Lintermann (2005).

## 2.1    RULE-BASED METHODS

Rule-based techniques make use of small sets of generative rules or a grammar to create branches and leaves. Prusinkiewicz et al. (1994, 1996), for example, developed a series of approaches based on the idea of the generative L-system. L-systems were introduced as a formalism for simulating the development of multicellular organs in terms of division, growth, and death of individual cells (Lindenmayer (1968)). An example of a plant that can be generated using such an L-system is shown in Figure 2.1. Extensions of the L-system have since been proposed to enhance its flexibility of use, e.g., adding the ability to handle physics (Noser et al. (2001)). See Section 2.7 for a brief introduction to L-systems.

On the other hand, de Reffye et al. (1988) used a collection of rules of plant growth to produce realistic-looking trees. The rules govern phenomena such as order of axis (axis is the stem or branch), phyllotaxy, and ramification process. See top row of Figure 2.2. The order of axis refers to the sequence of growth; order 1 grows out of the seed, and order $i$ axes ($i > 1$) grow from axillary buds of order $i - 1$ axes. Phyllotaxy refers to the relative arrangements of leaves along a branch. The arrangement can be spiraled or distic (planar symmetry). Ramification process refers to the type of branching that can be continuous (all growth is from every node along the axis), rhythmic (growth is from a fraction of the nodes), or diffuse (growth is from a random set of nodes). The general trend of growth is called plagiotropic if it is horizontal and orthotropic if vertical. To break total symmetry of growth, the growth of each bud is probabilistic. The user has to specify parameters such as age, growth speeds of axes, number of possible buds at each node, and various probabilities associated with death, pause, and ramification. Four tree models generated using this technique are shown in the bottom row of Figure 2.2.

**Figure 2.1:** Palm tree generated using an early version of L-system (from Prusinkiewicz et al. (1996)). Here the L-system simulates creation of new leaves at the apex of the trunk while old leaves are shed at the base of the crown using the cut operation (introduced in Hanan (1992)). Courtesy of P. Prusinkiewicz. Copyright © 1996 CSIRO.

Weber and Penn (1995) used a series of geometric rules to create results such as those shown in Figure 2.3. In their system, the tree consists of a primary trunk with a variably curved structure similar to a cone. The user specifies a number of parameters to control the shape of the tree; such parameters include general tree shape (include size and scale), levels of branch recursion, amount of branch tapering along its length, and stem parameters (splits at base of trunk, angle per segment). There are also parameters to specify global pruning to constrain the overall tree shape. Some of the tree parameters are depicted at the top of Figure 2.3. Please refer to their paper to get the exact meanings of the parameters shown in the figure.

Such rule-based techniques provide some realism and editability, but they require expertise for effective use, especially for the system of de Reffye et al. (1988). They work on the (usually) reasonable assumption that the branch shape and leaf arrangement follow a predictable pattern. On the other hand, they require considerable effort to replicate unexpected local structural modifications such as stunted growth due to disease or responses to external agents.

In addition to parameterized algorithms (Oppenheimer (1986); de Reffye et al. (1988); Holton (1994); Weber and Penn (1995)), combined approaches such as the xfrog system

**Figure 2.2:** Tree generation using plant growth rules. Top row (adapted from de Reffye et al. (1988)): order of axis, phyllotaxy, and ramification. Bottom row: results from de Reffye et al. (1988). From left to right: pine tree, wild cherry tree with fruits, coconut tree, and weeping willow. Photos courtesy of P. de Reffye. Copyright © 1988 ACM.

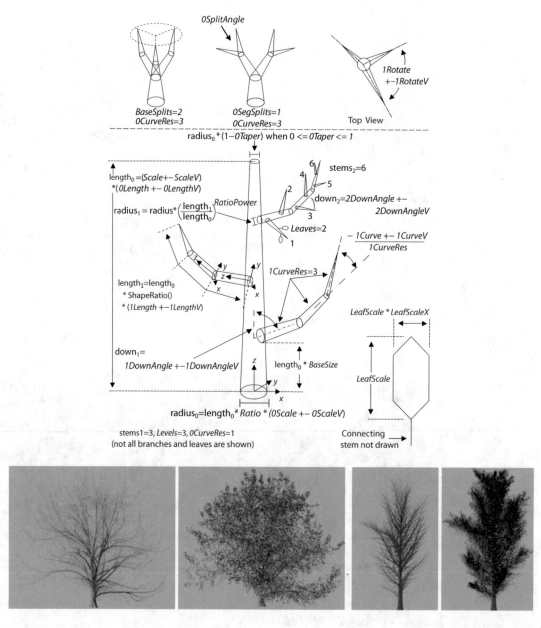

**Figure 2.3:** Rule-based generation of trees. Top: depiction of parameters used. Bottom: sample of trees generated using these parameters (from Weber and Penn (1995)). Courtesy of J. Weber. Copyright © 1995 ACM.

(Lintermann and Deussen (1999)) have also been proposed. The xfrog interface and sample results are shown in Figure 2.4. Regardless, all these rule-based systems require the user to manually fine tune a number of parameters in order to create the desired model.

**Figure 2.4:** Snapshots from the xfrog system (from Lintermann and Deussen (1999)). The interface is shown on the far left; it lists parameters the user can manipulate to control the shape and appearance of the plant. The spline box shown in the interface allows the user to control the shape of the leaf. On the right is a tree generated using xfrog's tree components. Courtesy of O. Deussen. Copyright © 1999 IEEE.

Rule-based systems are difficult for the novice user to operate because they require specialized knowledge of biomechanics and biology for effective parameter specification. The user must also understand how the rules are applied or even formulated evenly. In a number of such systems, the global shape of trees is difficult to control—slight changes in the local rules may result in significant changes in the global shape.

The xfrog system (shown in Figure 2.4) and subsequent graphical L-system editors (Power et al. (1999); Prusinkiewicz et al. (2001); Onishi et al. (2003); Ijiri et al. (2006)) allow the user to manipulate complex parameters graphically. Despite the increased ease of use, most of such systems still require the user to specify the less intuitive function plots, curves, and surface parameters that govern appearance (which are separate from the model shape). One exception is the sketch-based system of Ijiri et al. (2006) (next section). Note that the system of Onishi et al. (2003) only modifies the plant shape and does not control its growth.

Boudon et al. (2003) proposed a global-to-local design approach for managing tree shape parameters. They introduced *decomposition graphs* as multiscale representations of plant structures and presented interactive tools for editing these decomposition graphs.

## 2.2    SKETCH-BASED METHODS

Sketch-based systems were developed to provide a more intuitive way of generating plant models. For example, the system of Okabe et al. (2005) reconstructs the 3D branching pattern from 2D drawn sketches in different views by maximizing distances between branches. They use additional gesture-based editing functions to add, delete, or cut branches. Moreover, example-based editing is supported to generate branches or leaves using some existing tree models. Their system also requires the user to draw many branches to describe detailed structures. Because their system does not support automatic propagation of branches, a complex tree would require extensive user interaction. Examples of their inputs and outputs are shown in Figure 2.5.

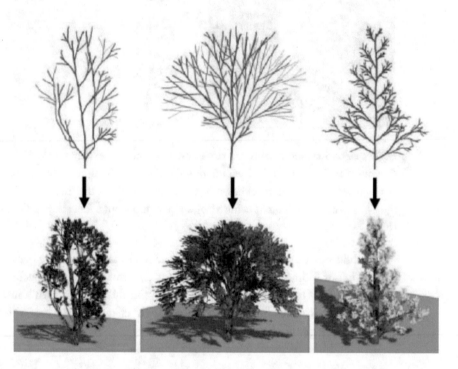

**Figure 2.5:** Examples of sketches and resulting 3D tree models (from Okabe et al. (2005)). Courtesy of M. Okabe. Copyright © 2005 Wiley Blackwell.

The system of Ijiri et al. (2006) is based on L-systems. The user draws a single free-form stroke to control the growth of a tree. The change in the shape of the stroke is used as a graphical metaphor for modifying the L-system parameters. However, this system supports only two simple production rules, and the user is not allowed to control the overall shape of the tree. This severely limits the expressive power of the system.

In comparison, the sketching system of Chen et al. (2008) generates a 3D tree model by having the user merely sketch the desired tree shape. The user does not need to understand what L-systems are or know what parameters need to be manipulated. While L-systems require parameters to be predefined and manipulated, their sketching system provides the user a highly intuitive way to produce the desired 3D tree models. Results from this system is shown in Figure 2.6.

As can be seen, the system of Chen et al. (2008) is capable of generating complex, natural-looking tree models from a limited number of strokes to describe the tree shape. The user can also define the overall shape of the tree by loosely sketching the contour of the crown.

The system described in Chapter 5 is also sketch-based. There are significant differences between these two systems. The sketching system described in Chapter 5 uses a tree image to guide the branch segmentation and leaf generation. It uses either the rule of maximal distance between branches (Okabe et al. (2005)) to convert 2D branches to their 3D counterparts or "elementary subtrees" whenever they are available. (The tree branches are generated through random selection and placement of the elementary subtrees.) Meanwhile, the sketching system of Chen et al. (2008) does not rely on an image but instead solves the inverse procedural modeling problem by inferring the generating parameters and 3D tree shape from the drawn sketch. The inference is guided by a database of exemplar trees with pre-computed growth parameters.

The system of Wither et al. (2009) is also sketch-based, but here the user sketches the silhouettes of foliage at multiple scales to generate the 3D model (as opposed to sketching all the branches). Botanical rules are applied to branches within each silhouette and between its main branch and the parent branch. The tree model can be very basic (simple enough for the novice user to generate) or each detailed part fully specified (for the expert).

## 2.3   IMAGE-BASED METHODS

Rather than requiring the user to manually specify the plant model, there are approaches that instead use images to help generate 3D models. They range from the use of a single image and (limited) shape priors (Han and Zhu (2003)) to multiple images (Sakaguchi (1998); Shlyakhter et al. (2001); Reche-Martinez et al. (2004)). The techniques we describe in this book (Chapters 3, 4, and (5) fall into the image-based category.

A popular approach is to use the visual hull to aid the modeling process (Sakaguchi (1998); Shlyakhter et al. (2001); Reche-Martinez et al. (2004)). While Shlyakhter et al. (2001) refines the medial axis of the volume to a simple L-system fit for branch generation, Sakaguchi (1998) uses simple branching rules in voxel space for the same purpose. However, the models generated by these approaches are only approximate and have limited realism.

Reche-Martinez et al. (2004), on the other hand, compute a volumetric representation with variable opacity (see Figure 2.7). Here, a set of carefully registered photographs is used to determine the volumetric shape and opacity of a given tree. The data is stored as a huge set of volume tiles and is, therefore, expensive to render and requires a significant amount of memory. While realism is achieved, their models cannot be edited or animated easily. Their follow-up work (Linz et al. (2006)) addresses the large data problem through efficient multi-resolution rendering and the use of vector quantization for texture compression.

Neubert et al. (2007) proposed a method to produce 3D tree models from several photographs based on limited user interaction. Their system is a combination of image-based and sketch-based modeling. From loosely registered input images, a voxel volume is achieved with density values which

**Figure 2.6:** Sample results for Chen et al. (2008). From left to right: sketch, reconstructed branch, complete branch structure, full tree model rendered at the same viewpoint as the input, and same tree model rendered from a different viewpoint.

**Figure 2.7:** Generating a voxel representation of a tree with variable opacity (from Reche-Martinez et al. (2004)). From left to right: an input image, the matte (used to compute opacity), two cross-sections of the estimated volumetric model with opacity, and textured volumetric model. Courtesy of G. Drettakis. Copyright © 2004 ACM.

are used to estimate an initial set of particles via an attactor graph (top row in Figure 2.8). For more visually pleasing results, the attractor graph is generated semi-automatically from user-selected seed points as guidance. A 3D flow simulation is performed to trace the particles downward to the tree basis. Finally, the twigs and branches are formed according to the particles. The user is required to draw some branches if there is no information about branching in the images. Density information is critical to simulate the particle. The user has to draw the foliage density if image information is missing. The final reconstructed branches do not have the exact same shape as the drawn branches. Figure 2.8 shows two sets of results using the technique of Neubert et al. (2007).

Xu et al. (2007) used a laser scanner to acquire the range data for modeling a tree. Part of our work described in Chapter 4—the generation of initial visible branches—is inspired by their work. The major difference is that they use a 3D point cloud for modeling; no registered source images are used. It is not easy to generate complete tree models from just 3D points because of the difficulties in determining what is missing and infilling the missing information. Our experience has led us to believe that adapting models to images is a more intuitive means for realistic modeling. The image-based approach is also more flexible for modeling a wide variety of trees at different scales.

Image-based approaches offer the greatest potential for producing realistic-looking plants since they rely on images of real plants. At the same time, they can produce only models of pre-existing plants. Designing new and visually-plausible plants is likely to be a non-trivial task.

## 2.4 MODELING LEAVES, FLOWERS, AND BARK

So far, the techniques that we reviewed are for generating the tree model at a macro level. There exist techniques for adding realistic detail to tree models, namely, leaves (Wang et al. (2005); Runions et al. (2005)), flowers (Ijiri et al. (2005, 2008)), and bark (Hart and Baker (1996); Lefebvre and Neyret (2002); Wang et al. (2003)). Such details are particularly important if close-ups of the models are expected.

**Figure 2.8:** Generating a tree model using images, sketch, and flow simulation (from Neubert et al. (2007)). First row: input image and estimated tree density (based on the input images) with attractor graph superimposed (in red). Second row: two input images and renderings of the extracted model. Third row: three input images, corresponding user-specified density via scribbles, and output model. Courtesy of O. Deussen. Copyright © 2007 ACM.

## 2.5    MODELING ENVIRONMENTAL EFFECTS

Brasch et al. (2007) developed an interactive visualization system for trees using growth data (which includes time-varying functions for the global tree dimensions, costs for tree upkeep, and benefits in terms of pollutant uptake and energy savings). It also simulates growth influenced by available light using quantized cuboids within the crown.

In Rudnick et al. (2007), the parameters of the local production rules are derived from global functions that describe the measured tree growth data over time. The production rules are influenced by the global light distribution, which is represented by the amount of light available at each position within the tree's crown.

The first simulation of the effect of light on plant growth was done by Greene (1989). The light effect was approximated using the sky hemisphere as a source of illumination that casts different amounts of light at different parts of the tree structures. A different variant was proposed by Kanamaru et al. (1992), who computed the amount of light reaching a given sampling point in a different manner. Here, the sampling point is considered a center of projection, from which all leaf clusters in a tree were projected onto the surrounding hemisphere. The amount of light received at the sampling point is proportional to how much the hemisphere was covered by the projected leaves. In both cases, the plant models simulate heliotropism by responding positively to the amount and direction of light.

Subsequent work on heliotropic simulation concentrated on more sophisticated tree models. For example, Chiba et al. (1994) extended the tree models by Kanamaru et al. (1992), including a mechanism simulating the flow of hypothetical endogenous information within the tree. Takenaka (1994) used a biologically better justified model that is formulated in terms of production and use of photosynthates by a tree. The amount of light reaching leaf clusters was calculated by sampling a sky hemisphere as in the work by Greene (1989).

There are other aspects of tree growth that were simulated. For instance, Liddell and Hansen (1993) modeled competition between root tips for nutrients and water transported in soil. Honda et al. (1981) simulated the competition for space (including collision detection and access to light) between segments of essentially two-dimensional schematic branching structures.

In another important development, Mech and Prusinkiewicz (1996) extended the formalism of Lindenmayer systems that allows the modeling of bi-directional information exchange between plants and their environment. Their proposed framework can handle collision-limited development and competition within and between plants for more favorable areas (light and water in soil).

More recently, Palubicki et al. (2009) proposed a technique for generating realistic models of temperate-climate trees and shrubs. Their technique is based on the competition of buds and branches for light or space. The outputs can be controlled with a variety of interactive techniques, including procedural brushes, sketching, and editing operations such as pruning and bending of branches. This technique is a good example of augmenting procedural tree modeling with interaction for refinement.

## 2.6   MODELING OTHER FLORA

Approaches for modeling flora other than the usual plants and trees do exist, though substantially fewer. There is work done on modeling grass (Boulanger et al. (2006); Perbet and Cani (2001)), and lower plants such as mushroom (Desbenoit et al. (2004)) and lichen (Sumner (2001); Desbenoit et al. (2004)). Such solutions tend to be more specialized.

## 2.7   APPENDIX: BRIEF DESCRIPTION OF L-SYSTEM

The L-system, or Lindenmayer system, is named after Aristid Lindenmayer (1925-1989). An L-system consists of a very terse grammar that is recursive; it reflects self-similarity that typifies the fractal-like plant and tree growth patterns. Mathematically, an L-system is defined by a grammar $G = (V, S, \omega, P)$, where $V$ is the set of variables (or replaceable symbols), $S$ the set of constants (or fixed symbols), $\omega$ a string that defines the initial state of the system (axiom), and $P$ the set of production rules. By applying $P$ to $\omega$ using $V$ and $S$, we produce the self-similar structure.

Here is a simple example: without defining what the variables represent, let us suppose that $F$ is a variable, $+$ and $-$ are constants, the rule is $F \rightarrow F + -F$, and the axiom (i.e., starting condition) is $F + F$. So, we have

Iteration 0: $F + F$
Iteration 1: $F + -F + F + -F$
Iteration 2: $F + -F + -F + -F + F + -F + -F + -F$

Notice that all we did was replace each instance of $F$ with $F + -F$ at every iteration. Notice also how quickly the number of variables grew at each iteration.

An L-system is characterized as:

- Context-free if each production rule is applied to *one* symbol independently of its neighbors.

- Context-sensitive if each production rule is applied to a symbol and its neighbors.

- Deterministic if each symbol has one production rule. If the L-system is deterministic *and* context-free, it is called a D0L-system.

- Stochastic if each symbol has several production rules which are applied probabilistically.

We now show an actual example of a L-system for generating a 3D tree model. For ease of illustration, we use the procedural metaphor of a turtle (Abelson and diSessa (1982)) moving in response to drawing commands (Prusinkiewicz (1986)). Let us define the following commands: $F$, $f$. Note that $F$, $f$ are variables while $+$, $-$ are constants. Also, [ and ] correspond to "pushing" the current state and "popping" the last-saved state of the system, respectively. All motion is relative to current position $\mathbf{p}$, transform $T$, and direction $\mathbf{t}$.

**Figure 2.9:** Examples of L-systems, with the same production rules but with different constants. Note that not all L-systems result in plausible-looking trees.

$F$ Move turtle in current direction $\mathbf{t}$ and draw: $\mathbf{p} \rightarrow \mathbf{p} + T\mathbf{t}$

$f$ Move turtle in current direction $\mathbf{t}$ without drawing: $\mathbf{p} \rightarrow \mathbf{p} + T\mathbf{t}$

$+$ Increase rotation about y-axis by $\delta_y$: $\mathbf{p} \rightarrow \mathbf{p} + TR_y(\delta_y)\mathbf{t}$

$-$ Decrease rotation about y-axis by $\delta_y$: $\mathbf{p} \rightarrow \mathbf{p} + TR_y(-\delta_y)\mathbf{t}$

$\#$ Increase rotation about z-axis by $\delta_z$: $\mathbf{p} \rightarrow \mathbf{p} + TR_z(\delta_z)\mathbf{t}$

$!$ Decrease rotation about z-axis by $\delta_z$: $\mathbf{p} \rightarrow \mathbf{p} + TR_z(-\delta_z)\mathbf{t}$

$\%$ Reduce branch diameter by ratio $b$

$|$ Reduce branch length by ratio $l$

The production rule is relatively simple:

$$F \rightarrow F[+\#|\%F][-!|\%F],$$

with the axiom being $F$, $T$ being the identity matrix, $\mathbf{p} = \mathbf{0}$, and $\mathbf{t} = (0, 1, 0)^\mathrm{T}$. The L-system above produced the examples shown in Figure 2.9. From left to right, the values $(\delta_y, \delta_z, b, l)$ are $(41°, 22°, 0.96, 0.98)$, $(2°, 22°, 0.96, 0.94)$, $(30°, 49°, 0.99, 0.88)$, and $(46°, 74°, 0.96, 0.86)$.

CHAPTER 3

# Image-Based Technique for Modeling Plants

In this chapter, we describe our system for modeling plants from images. As indicated in Chapter 1, this system is designed to model flora with relatively large leaves; the shapes of these leaves are extracted from images as part of the modeling process.

## 3.1 OVERVIEW OF PLANT MODELING SYSTEM

There are three parts in our system: image acquisition and structure from motion, leaf segmentation and recovery, and interactive branch recovery. The system is summarized in Figure 3.1.

We use a hand-held camera to capture images of the plant at different views. We then apply a standard structure from motion technique to recover the camera parameters and a 3D point cloud.

Next, we segment the 3D data points and 2D images into individual leaves. To facilitate this process, we designed a simple interface that allows the user to specify the segmentation jointly using 3D data points and 2D images. The data to be partitioned is represented as a 3D undirected weighted graph that gets updated on-the-fly. For a given plant to model, the user first segments out a leaf; this is used as a deformable generic model. This generic leaf model is subsequently used to fit the other segmented data to model all the other visible leaves. Our system is also designed to use the images as guides for interactive reconstruction of the branches.

The resulting model of the plant very closely resembles the appearance and complexity of the real plant. Just as important, because the output is a geometric model, it can be easily manipulated or edited.

## 3.2 PRELIMINARY PROCESSES

Image acquisition is simple: the user just uses a hand-held camera to capture the appearance of the plant of interest from a number of different overlapping views. The main caveat during the capture process is that appearance changes due to changes in lighting and shadows should be avoided. For all the experiments reported in this chapter, we used between 30 to 45 input images taken around each plant.

Prior to any user-assisted geometry reconstruction, we extract point correspondences and ran structure from motion on them to recover camera parameters and a collection of 3D points. Standard computer vision techniques have been developed to estimate the point correspondences across the images and the camera parameters (Hartley and Zisserman (2000); Faugeras et al. (2001)). We used

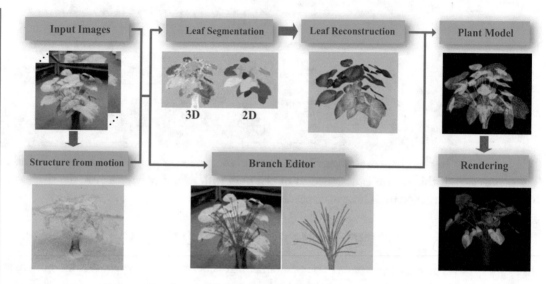

**Figure 3.1:** Overview of our image-based plant modeling approach.

the approach described in Lhuillier and Quan (2005) to compute a quasi-dense cloud of reliable 3D points in space. This technique is used because it has been shown to be robust and capable of providing sufficiently dense point clouds for depicting objects. This technique is well-suited because plants tend to be highly textured.

The quasi-dense feature points used in Lhuillier and Quan (2005) are not the points of interest (Hartley and Zisserman (2000)), but regularly re-sampled image points from a kind of disparity map. One example is shown in Figure 3.1. We are typically able to obtain about a hundred thousand 3D points that unsurprisingly tend to cluster at textured areas. These points help by delineating the shape of the plant. Each 3D point is associated with images where it was observed; this book-keeping is useful in segmenting leaves and branches during the modeling cycle.

## 3.3 GRAPH-BASED LEAF EXTRACTION

We next proceed to recover the geometry of the individual leaves. This is clearly a difficult problem, due to the similarity of color between different overlapping leaves. To minimize the amount of user interaction, we formulate the leaf segmentation problem as interactive graph-based optimization aided by 3D and 2D information. The graph-based technique simultaneously partitions 3D points and image pixels into discrete sets, with each set representing a leaf. We bring the user into the loop to make the segmentation process more efficient and robust.

One unique feature of our system is the joint use of 2D and 3D data to allow simple user assist as all our images and 3D data are perfectly registered. The process is not manually intensive as we only need to have one image segmentation for each leaf. This is because the leaf reconstruction algorithm (see Section 3.4) needs only one image segmentation boundary per leaf. This is sub-optimal but substantially more efficient.

There are two main steps to the segmentation process: automatic segmentation by a graph partition algorithm, followed by user interaction to refine the segmentation. Our system responds to user input by immediately updating the graph and image boundaries.

### 3.3.1    GRAPH PARTITION

The weighted graph $G = \{V, E\}$ is built by taking each 3D point as a node and connecting it to its K-nearest neighboring points (K=3) with edges. The K-nearest neighbor is computed using 3D Euclidean distance, and each connecting edge should at least be visible at one view. The weight on each edge reflects the likelihood that the two points being connected belong to the same leaf. We define a combined distance function for a pair of points (nodes) $p$ and $q$ as

$$d(p, q) = (1 - \alpha)\frac{d_{3D}(p, q)}{\sqrt{2}\sigma_{3D}} + \alpha\frac{d_{2D}(p, q)}{\sqrt{2}\sigma_{2D}},$$

where $\alpha$ is a weighting scalar set to 0.5 by default. The 3D distance $d_{3D}(p, q)$ is the 3D Euclidean distance, with $\sigma_{3D}$ being its variance. The 2D distance measurement, computed over all observed views, is

$$d_{2D}(p, q) = \max_{i}\{ \max_{u_i \in [p_i, q_i]} g_i(u_i)\}.$$

The interval $[p_i, q_i]$ specifies the line segment joining the projections of $p$ and $q$ on the $i$th image. $u_i$ is an image point on this line segment. The function $g(\cdot)$ is the color gradient along the line segment; it is approximated using color difference between adjacent pixels. $\sigma_{2D}$ is the variance of the color gradient. The weight of a graph edge is defined as $w(p, q) = e^{-d^2(p,q)}$.

The initial graph partition is obtained by thresholding the weight function $w(\cdot)$ with $k$ set to 3 by default,

$$w(p, q) = \begin{cases} e^{-d^2(p,q)}, & \text{if } d_{3D} < k\sigma_{3D} \text{ and } d_{2D} < k\sigma_{2D}, \\ 0, & \text{otherwise.} \end{cases}$$

This produces groups that are clearly different. However, at this point, the partitioning is typically coarse, requiring further subdivision for each group. We use the normalized cut approach described in Shi and Malik (2000). The normalized cut computation is efficient in our case as the initial graph partition significantly reduces the size of each subgraph, and the weight matrix is sparse as it has at most $(2K + 1)N$ non-zero elements for a graph of $N$ nodes for $K$-nearest neighbors. This approach is effective due to the joint use of 2D and 3D information. Figure 3.2 shows that if only 3D distance is used ($\alpha = 0$), a collection of leaves are segmented but not individual ones. When images are used ($\alpha = 0.5$) as well, each collection is further partitioned into individual leaves using edge point information.

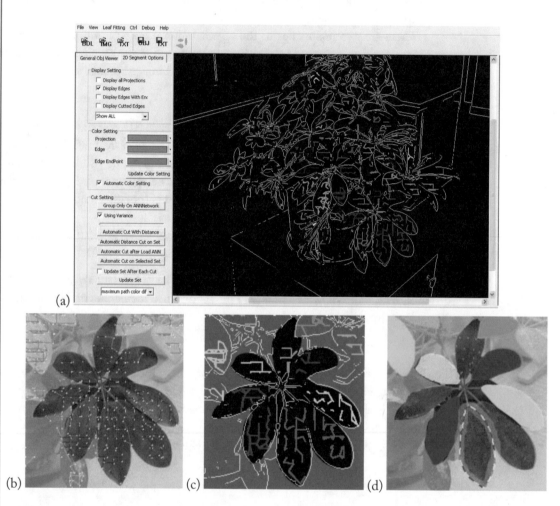

**Figure 3.2:**  Benefit of jointly using 3D and 2D information. (a) Interface. Closeups are shown in (b)-(d). (b) The projection of visible 3D points (in yellow) and connecting edges (in red) are superimposed on an input image. Using only 3D distance resulted in coarse segmentation of the leaves. (c) The projection of segmented 3D points with only the connecting edges superimposed on the gradient image (in white). A different color is used to indicate a different group of connecting edges. Using both 3D and 2D image gradient information resulted in segmentation of leaflets. (d) Automatically generated leaflets are shown as solid-colored regions. The user drew the rough boundary region (thick orange line) to assist segmentation, which relabels the red points and triggers a graph update. The leaflet boundary is then automatically extracted (dashed curve).

### 3.3.2   USER INTERFACE

In general, the process of segmentation is subjective; the segments that represent different objects depend on the person's perception of what an object is. In the case of partitioning the image into leaves, while the interpretation is much clearer, the problem is nonetheless still very difficult. This is because leaves in the same plant look very similar, and boundaries between overlapping leaves are often very subtle.

We designed simple ways the user can help refine areas where automatic segmentation fails. In the interface, each current 3D group is projected into the image as a feedback mechanism. The user can modify the segmentation and obtain the image boundary segmentation in any of the following ways:

- **Click to confirm segmentation.** The user can click on an image region to indicate that the current segmentation group is acceptable. This operation triggers 2D boundary segmentation, described in Section 3.3.4.

- **Draw to split and refine.** The user can draw a rough boundary to split the group and refine the boundary. This operation triggers two actions: First, it cuts off the connecting edges crossing the marked boundary, so that points inside the boundary are relabelled, which in turn causes an update of the graph partition by splitting the group into two subgroups. The graph updating method is described in Section 3.3.3. Second, it triggers 2D boundary segmentation.

- **Click to merge.** The user can click on two points to create an connecting edge to merge the two subgroups.

### 3.3.3   GRAPH UPDATE

The graph update for affected groups is formulated as a two-label graph-cut problem (Boykov et al. (2001)) that minimizes the following energy function:

$$E(l) = \sum_l (1 - \delta(l_p, l_q)) \frac{1}{d^2(p, q) + \epsilon} + \sum_l D(l_p),$$

where $\delta(l_p, l_q)$ is 1 if $l_p = l_q$, 0 if $l_p \neq l_q$, and $l_p, l_q = \{0, 1\}$. $\epsilon$ is a very small positive constant set to 0.0001. The data term $D(\cdot)$ encodes the user-confirmed labels:

$$\begin{cases} D(0) = 0, \\ D(1) = \infty, \end{cases} \text{if } l_p = 0 \text{ and } \begin{cases} D(0) = \infty, \\ D(1) = 0, \end{cases} \text{if } l_p = 1.$$

It is implemented as a min-cut algorithm that produces a global minimum (Boykov et al. (2001)). The complexity of the min-cut is $O(N^3)$, with $N$ nodes and at most $5N$ edges for our graph. Since each group is usually rather small (a few thousand nodes), the update is immediate, allowing the interface to provide real-time visual feedback.

### 3.3.4   BOUNDARY SEGMENTATION

The image segmentation for a given group of 3D points in a given image is also solved as a two-way graph-cut problem, this time using a 2D graph (not the graph for our 3D points) built with pixels as nodes. Our segmentation algorithm is similar to that of Li et al. (2004). However, for our algorithm, the foreground and background are automatically computed as opposed to being supplied by the user in Li et al. (2004).

The foreground is defined as the entire region covered by the projected 3D points in a group. The background consists of the projections of all other points not in the group currently being considered. As was done in Li et al. (2004), we oversegment each image using the watershed algorithm in order to reduce the complexity of processing. Any reference to the image is actually a pointer to a color segment rather than to a pixel.

Note that a more automated segmentation technique is described in Quan et al. (2007). It is based on the same principle of joint 2D-3D segmentation. However, it is still prone to errors, which require the user to correct.

## 3.4   MODEL-BASED LEAF RECONSTRUCTION

Since leaves in the same plant are typically very similar, we adopt the strategy of extracting a generic leaf model from a sample leaf and using it to fit all the other leaves. This strategy turns out to be more robust as it reduces uncertainty due to noise and occlusion by constraining the shapes of leaves.

### 3.4.1   EXTRACTION OF A GENERIC LEAF MODEL

To extract a generic leaf model, the user manually chooses an example leaf from its most fronto-parallel view as shown in Figure 3.3. The texture and boundary associated with the leaf are taken to be the flat model of the leaf. The leaf model consists of three polylines: two for the leaf boundary and one for the central vein. Each polyline is represented by about 10 vertices. The leaf model is expressed in a local Euclidean coordinate frame with the $x-$axis being the major axis. The region inside the boundary is triangulated; the model is automatically subdivided to increase the accuracy of the model, depending on the density of points in the group.

### 3.4.2   LEAF RECONSTRUCTION

Leaf reconstruction consists of four steps: generic flat leaf fit, 3D boundary warping, shape deformation, followed by texture assignment.

**Flat leaf fit.**   We start by fitting the generic *flat* leaf model to the group of 3D points. This is done by computing the principal components of the data points of the group via singular value decomposition (SVD). A flat leaf is reconstructed at the local coordinate frame determined by the first two components of the 3D points. Then, the flat leaf is scaled in two directions by mapping it to the model. The recovered flat leaves are shown in Figure 3.3(a).

(a)                                                                                          (b)

**Figure 3.3:** Leaf reconstruction for poinsettia (Figure 3.6). (a) Reconstructed flat leaves using 3D points. The generic leaf model is shown at top right. (b) Leaves after deforming using image boundary and closest 3D points.

There is, however, an orientation ambiguity for the flat leaf. Note that this orientation ambiguity does not affect the whole geometry reconstruction procedure described in this section, so that the ambiguity is not critical at this point. A leaf is usually facing up and away from a branch. We use this heuristic to find the orientation of the leaf, i.e., facing up and away from the vertical axis going through the centroid of the whole plant. For a complicated branching structure, the leaf orientations may be incorrect. Once the branches have been reconstructed (Section 3.5), the system will automatically recompute the leaf orientation using information from the branching structure.

**Leaf boundary warping.**   While the 3D points of a leaf are adequate for locating its pose and approximate shape, they do not completely specify the leaf boundary. This is where boundary information obtained from the images is used. Each group of 3D points are associated with 2D image segmentations at different views (if such segmentation exists). A leaf boundary will not be refined if there is no corresponding image segmentation for the leaf. On the other hand, if multiple regions (across multiple views) exist for a leaf, the largest region is used.

Once the 3D leaf plane has been recovered, we back-project the image boundary onto the leaf plane. We look for the best affine transformation that maps the flat leaf to the image boundary by minimizing the distances between the two sets of points of the boundaries on the leaf plane in space. We adapted the ICP (Iterative Closest-Point) algorithm (Besl and McKay (1992)) to compute the registration of two curve boundaries. We first compute a global affine transformation using the first two components of the SVD decomposition as the initial transformation. Correspondences are established by assigning each leaf boundary point to the closest image boundary; these correspondences are used to re-estimate the affine transformation. The procedure stops when the mean distance between the two sets of points falls below a threshold.

**Shape deformation.**   The final shape of the leaf is obtained by locally deforming the flat leaf in directions perpendicular to the plane to fit the nearest 3D points. This adds shape detail to the leaf (Figure 3.3(b)).

**Texture reconstruction.**   The texture of each leaf first inherits that of the generic model. The texture from the image segmentation is subsequently used to overwrite the default texture. This is done to ensure that occluded or slightly misaligned parts are textured.

## 3.5   BRANCH EXTRACTION AND RECONSTRUCTION

Once the leaves have been reconstructed, the next step would be to reconstruct the branches to complete the plant model. Unfortunately, the branching structure is difficult to reconstruct automatically from images due to occlusion and segmenting difficulties similar to those for leaves. One possible approach would be to use rules or grammar (L-systems). However, it is not clear how these can be used to fit partial information closely or how the novice user can exercise *local* control to edit the 3D branches (say, in occluded areas).

Our solution is to design a data-driven editor that allows the user to easily recover the branch structure. We model each branch as a generalized cylinder, with the skeleton being a 3D spline curve. The cylindrical radius can be spatially varying. It is specified at each endpoint of each branch, and linearly interpolated between the endpoints. While the simple scheme may not follow specific botanical models, it is substantially more flexible and easier to handle—and it can be used to closely model the observed plant.

The user is presented with an interface with two areas: an area showing the current synthesized tree (optionally with 3D points and/or leaves as overlay), and the other showing the synthetic tree superimposed on an input image. The image can be switched to any other input image at any time. User operations can be performed in any one area, with changes propagated to the other area in real-time as feedback. There are four basic operations the user can perform:

- **Draw curve.** The user can draw a curve from any point of an existing branch to create the next level branch. If the curve is drawn in 3D, the closest existing 3D points are used to trace a branch. If drawn in 2D, at each point in the curve, its 3D coordinate is assigned to be the 3D point whose projection is the closest. If the closest points having 3D information are too far away, the 3D position is inherited from its parent branch.

- **Move curve.** The user can move a curve by clicking on any point of the current branch to a new position.

 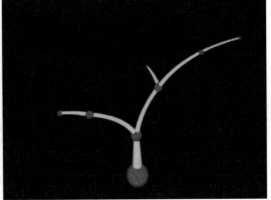

**Figure 3.4:** Branch structure editing. The editable areas are shown: 2D area (left), 3D space (right). The user modifies the radii of the circles or spheres (shown in red) to change the thickness of branches.

- **Edit radius.** The radius is indicated as a circle (in 2D) or a sphere (in 3D). The user can enlarge or shrink the circle or sphere directly on the interface, effectively increasing or reducing the radius, respectively.

- **Specify leaf.** The user can specify if each branch can grow a leaf at its endpoint (see the green branches in Figure 3.4). A synthesized leaf will be the average leaf over all reconstructed leaves, scaled by the thickness of the branch.

Once the branching structure is finalized, each leaf is automatically connected to the nearest branch. The orientation of each leaf, initially determined using a heuristic, as described in Section 3.3, is also automatically refined at this stage. The plant model is produced by assembling all the reconstructed branches and leaves.

## 3.6    RESULTS

We have reconstructed a variety of plants with different shapes and densities of foliage. In this section, we show results for four different plants: nephthytis, poinsetta, schefflera, and an indoor tree. Because of variation in leaf shape, size, and density, the level of difficulty for each example is different. We typically capture about 35 images, more for plants with smaller leaves (specifically the indoor tree). The captured image resolution is $1944 \times 2592$ (except for the poinsettia, which is $1200 \times 1600$). For the efficiency of structure from motion, we down-sampled the images to $583 \times 777$ (for the poinsettia, to $600 \times 800$). It took approximately 10 mins for about 40 images on a 1.9GHz P4 PC with 1 GB of RAM. On average, we reconstructed about 30,000 3D points for the foreground plant.

The recovered texture-mapped geometry models are rendered using Maya to produce images shown in this chapter. The statistics associated with the reconstructions are summarized in Table 3.1.

**Figure 3.5:** An indoor tree. Left: an input image (out of 45). Right: the recovered model, inserted into a simple synthetic scene.

About 80 percent of the leaves were automatically recovered by our system. Figure 3.5 shows a simple example of inserting the reconstructed model into a synthetic scene. We also show examples of plant editing: texture replacement (Figure 3.6), and branch and leaf cut-and-paste (Figure 3.7).

**Nephthytis.**   This plant has large broad leaves, which makes modeling easy. The 3D points are accurate, and leaf extraction and recovery are fairly straightforward. Only the extraction of 6 leaves are assisted by the user, and the reconstruction is fully automatic. The 3D points were sufficient in characterizing the spatial detail of the leaf shapes, as shown in Figure 3.8.

**Poinsettia and schefflera.**   These plants have medium sized leaves; as a result, the recovered 3D points on leaves were still of high quality. Occlusion is difficult when the foliage is dense, and the foliage for the poinsettia (see Figure 3.6) and schefflera is denser than that of the nephthytis. Leaf segmentation of the schefflera is complicated by the overlapping leaves and the small leaves at the tip of branches. We recovered about two-thirds of all possible leaves and synthesized some of them (on the top most branch) using the branching structure, as shown in Figure 3.7.

(a)

(b)

(c)

(d)

**Figure 3.6:** Image-based modeling of poinsettia plant. (a) An input image out of 35 images, (b) recovered model rendered at the same viewpoint as (a), (c) recovered model rendered at a different viewpoint, (d) recovered model with modified leaf textures.

**Figure 3.7:** Schefflera plant. Top left: an input image (out of 40 images). Top right: recovered model with synthesized leaves rendered at the same viewpoint as the top left. Bottom right: recovered model from images only. The white rectangles show where the synthesized leaves were added in the top right. Bottom left: recovered model after some geometry editing.

Table 3.1: Reconstruction statistics. The foreground points are automatically computed as the largest connected component in front of the cameras; they include both the plant, pot, and sometimes part of the floor. The segmentation parameters $\alpha$ and $k$ are defined in Section 3.3.1. Note: FG = foreground, AL = automatic leaves, UAL = user assisted leaves, ASL = additional synthetic leaves, BET = branch edit time.

|  | nephthytis | poinsettia | schefflera | indoor tree |
|---|---|---|---|---|
| # Images | 35 | 35 | 40 | 45 |
| # 3D pts | 128,000 | 103,000 | 118,000 | 156,000 |
| # FG pts | 53,000 | 83,000 | 43,000 | 31,000 |
| # Leaves | 30 | $\approx$120 | $\approx$450 | $\approx$1500 |
| $(\alpha, k)$ | (0,3) | (0.5,3) | (0.5,3) | (0.3,2) |
| # AL | 23 | 85 | 287 | 509 |
| # UAL | 6 | 21 | 69 | 35 |
| # ASL | 0 | 10 | 18 | 492 |
| All leaves | 29 | 116 | 374 | 1036 |
| BET (min) | 5 | 2 | 15 | 40 |

**Indoor tree.**   The indoor tree, with its small leaves, was the most difficult to model. First, the 3D points are less accurate because they were typically recovered from 2D points on occluding boundaries of leaves (which are not reliable). In addition, much more user interaction was required to recover the branching structure due to its high complexity. The segmentation was fully automatic using a smaller $k = 2$. For each group containing more than 3 points, the same automatic leaf fitting procedure is used. The exception is the generic model, which is much simpler. However, the geometric accuracy of the orientation of the recovered leaves is noticeably less reliable than that of the large leaves in the other examples. If the group contains fewer than 3 points, it is no longer possible to compute the pose of the leaf. In this case, the pose of each leaf was heuristically determined using geometry information of its nearest branch. A tree like this is better modeled using the technique described in the next chapter.

## 3.7   DISCUSSION

There are several possible straightforward improvements to our current implementation. For instance, the graph-based segmentation algorithm could be made more efficient by incorporating more priors based on real examples. Our current leaf reconstruction involves shape interpolation using the precomputed 3D points; better estimates may be obtained by referring to the original images during this process. Also, we use only one 2D boundary to refine the shape of the 3D leaf model. It may be more robust to incorporate the boundaries from multiple views instead. However, occlusions

**Figure 3.8:** Nephthytis plant. An input image out of 35 images on the left, and recovered model rendered at the same viewpoint as the image on the left. See also Figure 3.1 for intermediate results.

are still a problem, and, accounting for multiple views, substantially complicates the optimization. A more complex model for handling complex-looking flowers could be built, as suggested by Ijiri et al. (2005). Finally, for enhanced realism, one can use specialized algorithms for rendering specific parts of the plant, e.g., leaf rendering (Wang et al. (2005)).

## 3.8   SUMMARY

We have proposed a general approach to modeling plants from images. The key idea is to combine both available reconstructed 3D points and the images to more effectively segment the data into individual leaves. To increase robustness, we use a generic leaf model (extracted from the same image dataset) to fit all the other leaves.

We also developed a user-friendly branch structure editor that is also guided by 3D and 2D information. The results demonstrate the effectiveness of our system. We designed our system to be easy to use; specialized knowledge about plant structure, while helpful, is not required. Note, however, that this technique is not designed for modeling trees with many small leaves. The next chapter describes another image-based system specifically designed to handle such cases.

# CHAPTER 4

# Image-Based Technique for Modeling Trees

The previous chapter describes a system for modeling plants. This system works reasonably well if the size of the leaves is significant relative to the plant. However, as the indoor tree example in the previous chapter illustrates, trees with relatively small leaves are substantially harder to model using this system.

In this chapter, we describe a modified system to specifically model trees. The capture process is the same, as is the initial preprocessing step of structure-from-motion. This is where the similarities end. The visible branches are modeled and replicated in places obscured by the leaves. The point cloud associated with the leaves is used to constrain the spatial extent of branch replication; the final leaves are generated by backprojecting the segmented leaves to the closest 3D branch. Again, our system is designed to require as little user interaction as possible.

To recap Chapter 1, we differentiate between plants and trees—we consider "plants" as terrestrial flora with large discernible leaves (relative to the plant size) and "trees" as large terrestrial flora with small leaves (relative to the tree size). The spectrum of plants and trees with varying leaf sizes is shown in Figure 4.1.

## 4.1 OVERVIEW OF THE SYSTEM

Our tree modeling system consists of three main parts: image capture and 3D point recovery, branch recovery, and leaf population, illustrated in Figure 4.2. It is designed to reduce the amount of user interaction required by using as much data from images as possible. The recovery of the visible branches is mostly automatic, with the user given the option of refining their shapes. The subsequent recovery of the occluded branches and leaves is automatic with only a few parameters to be set by the user.

As was done by researchers in the past, we capitalize on the structural regularity of trees, more specifically the self-similarity of structural patterns of branches and the arrangement of leaves. However, rather than extracting rule parameters (which is very difficult to do in general), we use the extracted local arrangement of visible branches as building blocks to generate the occluded ones. This is done using the recovered 3D points as hard constraints and the matte silhouettes of trees in the source images as soft constraints.

To populate the tree with leaves, the user first provides the expected average image footprint of leaves. The system then segments each source image based on color. The 3D position of each leaf segment is determined either by its closest 3D point or by its closest branch segment. The

Plants with large
discernible leaves

Trees with small
undiscernible leaves

**Chapter 3** ⟶

*Increasingly more
manual intensive*

⟵

*Increasingly less
similar to inputs*

**This chapter**

**Figure 4.1:** Spectrum of plants and trees based on relative leaf size: on the left end of the spectrum, the size of the leaves relative to the plant is large. This is ideal for using the modeling system described in Chapter 3. The modeling system described in this chapter, on the other hand, targets trees with small relative leaf sizes (compared to the entire tree).

Source Images ⟶ Structure from motion ⟶ Reconstruction of visible branches ⟶ Reconstruction of occluded branches ⟶ Image Segmentation ⟶ Textured 3D model

**Figure 4.2:** Overview of our tree modeling system.

orientation of each leaf is approximated from the shape of the region relative to the leaf model or the best-fit plane of leaf points in its vicinity.

## 4.2    IMAGE CAPTURE AND 3D POINT RECOVERY

We use a hand-held camera to capture the appearance of the tree of interest from a number of different overlapping views. In all but one of our experiments, only 10 to 20 images were taken for each tree, with coverage between 120° and 200° around the tree. The exception is the potted flower tree shown in Figure 4.7 where 32 images covering 360° were taken.

Prior to any user-assisted geometry reconstruction, we extract point correspondences and ran structure from motion on them to recover camera parameters and a 3D point cloud. We also assume the matte for the tree has been extracted in each image, so that we know the extracted 3D point cloud is that of the tree and not the background. In our implementation, matting is achieved with automatic color-based segmentation and some user guidance.

Standard computer vision techniques have been developed to estimate the point correspondences across the images and the camera parameters. We used the approach described in Lhuillier and Quan (2005) to compute the camera poses and a quasi-dense cloud of reliable 3D points in space. Depending on the spatial distribution of the camera and the geometric complexity of the tree, there may be significant areas that are missing or sparse due to occlusion. One example of structure from motion is shown in Figure 4.2.

## 4.3    BRANCH RECOVERY

Once the camera poses and 3D point cloud have been extracted, we next reconstruct the tree branches, starting with the visible ones. The local structures of the visible branches are subsequently used to reconstruct those that are occluded in a manner similar to non-parametric texture synthesis in 2D (Efros and Leung (1999), and later 3D, Breckon and Fisher (2005)), using the 3D points as constraints.

To enable the branch recovery stage to be robust, we make three assumptions. First, we assume that the cloud of 3D points has been partitioned into points belonging to the branches and leaves (using color and position). Second, the tree trunk and its branches are assumed to be unoccluded. Finally, we expect the structures of the visible branches to be highly representative of those that are occluded (modulo some scaled rigid transform).

### 4.3.1    RECONSTRUCTION OF VISIBLE BRANCHES

The cloud of 3D points associated with the branches is used to guide the reconstruction of visible branches. Note that these 3D points can be in the form of multiple point clusters due to occlusion of branches. We call each cluster a *branch cluster*; each branch cluster has a primary branch with the rest being secondary branches.

The visible branches are reconstructed using a data-driven, bottom-up approach with a reasonable amount of user interaction. The reconstruction starts with graph construction, with each sub-graph representing a branch cluster. The user clicks on a 3D point of the primary branch to initiate the process. Once the reconstruction is done, the user iteratively selects another branch cluster to be reconstructed in very much the same way until all the visible branches are accounted for. The very first branch cluster handled consists of the tree trunk (primary branch) and its branches (secondary branches).

There are two parts to the process of reconstructing visible branches: graph construction to find the branch clusters, followed by sub-graph refinement to extract structure from each branch cluster.

**Graph construction.**    Given the 3D points and 3D-2D projection information, we build a graph G by taking each 3D point as a node and connecting it to its neighboring points with edges. The neighboring points are all those points whose distance to a given point is smaller than a threshold set by the user. The weight associated with each edge between a pair of points is a combined distance $d(p, q) = (1 - \alpha)d_{3D} + \alpha d_{2D}$ with $\alpha = 0.5$ by default. The 3D distance $d_{3D}$ is the 3D Euclidean distance between $p$ and $q$ normalized by its variance. For each image $I_i$ that $p$ and $q$ project to, let $l_i$ be the resulting line segment in the image joining their projections $\mathcal{P}_i(p)$ and $\mathcal{P}_i(q)$. Also, let $n_i$ be the number of pixels in $l_i$ and $\{x_{ij} | j = 1, ..., n_i\}$ be the set of 2D points in $l_i$. We define a 2D distance function $d_{2D} = \sum_i \frac{1}{n_i} \sum_j |\nabla I_i(x_{ij})|$, normalized by its variance, with $\nabla I(x)$ being the gradient in image $I$ at 2D location $x$. The 2D distance function accounts for the normalized intensity variation along the projected line segments over all observed views. If the branch in the source images has been identified and pre-segmented (e.g., using some semi-automatic segmentation technique), this function is set to infinity if any line segment is projected outside the branch area. Each connected component, or sub-graph, is considered as a branch cluster. We now describe how each branch cluster is processed to produce geometry, which consists of the skeleton and its thickness distribution.

**Conversion of sub-graph into branches.**    We start with the branch cluster that contains the lowest 3D point (the "root" point), which we assume to be part of the primary branch. (For the first cluster, the primary branch is the tree trunk.) The shortest paths from the root point to all other points are computed by a standard shortest path algorithm. The edges of the sub-graph are kept if they are part of the shortest paths and discarded otherwise.

This step results in 3D points linked along the surface of branches. Next, to extract the skeleton, the lengths of the shortest paths are divided into segments of a pre-specified length. The centroid of the points in each segment is computed and is referred to as a skeleton node. The radius of this node (or the radius of the corresponding branch) is the standard deviation of the points in the same bin. This procedure is similar to those described in Xu et al. (2007) and Brostow et al. (2004).

**User interface for branch refinement.**    Our system allows the user to refine the branches through simple operations that include adding or removing skeleton nodes, inserting a node between two adjacent nodes, and adjusting the radius of a node (which controls the local branch thickness). In addition, the user can also connect different branch clusters by clicking on one skeleton node of one cluster and a root point of another cluster. The connection is used to guide the creation of occluded branches that link these two clusters (see Section 4.3.2). Another feature of our system is that all these operations can be specified at a view corresponding to any one of the source images; this allows user interaction to occur with the appropriate source image superimposed for reference.

A result of branch structure recovery is shown for the bare tree example in Figure 4.3. This tree was captured with 19 images covering about 120°. The model was automatically generated from only one branch cluster.

**Figure 4.3:**  Bare tree example. From left to right: one of the source images, superimposed branch-only tree model, and branch-only tree model rendered at a different viewpoint.

## 4.3.2    RECONSTRUCTION OF OCCLUDED BRANCHES

The recovery of visible branches serves two purposes: portions of the tree model are reconstructed, and *the reconstructed parts are used to replicate the occluded branches*. We make the important assumption that the tree branch structure is locally self-similar. In our current implementation, any subset, i.e., a subtree, of the recovered visible branches is a candidate replication block. This is illustrated in Figure 4.4 for the final branch results shown in Figures 4.6 and 4.7.

The next step is to recover the occluded branches given the visible branches and the library of replication blocks. We treat this problem as texture synthesis, with the visible branches providing the texture sample and boundary conditions. There is a major difference with conventional texture synthesis: the scaling of a replication block is spatially dependent. This is necessary to ensure that the generated branches are geometrically plausible with the visible branches.

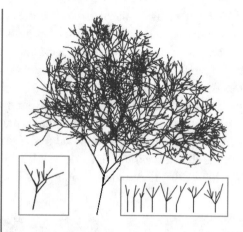
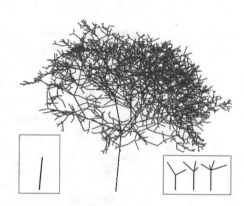

**Figure 4.4:**  Branch reconstruction for two different trees: fig tree in Figure 4.6 (left) and potted flower tree in Figure 4.7 (right). For each sub-figure: bottom left is the skeleton associated with visible branches and bottom right shows representative replication blocks. (Note that only the trunk of the potted flower tree is clearly visible. Three replication blocks were taken from another tree and used for branch reconstruction.)

In a typical tree with dense foliage, most of branches in the upper crown are occluded. To create plausible branches in this area, the system starts from the existing branches and "grows" to occupy part of the upper crown using our synthesis approach. The cut-off boundaries are specified by the tree silhouettes from the source images. The growth of the new branches can also be influenced by the reconstructed 3D points on the tree surface as branch endpoints. Depending on the availability of reconstructed 3D points, the "growth" of occluded branches can be unconstrained or constrained.

**Unconstrained growth.**    In areas where 3D points are unavailable, the system randomly picks an endpoint or a node of a branch structure and attaches the endpoint or node to a random replication block. Although the branch selection is mostly random, priority is given to thicker branches or those closer to the tree trunk. In growing the branches, two parameters associated with the replication block are computed on the fly: a random rotation and a scale. The replication block is first rotated about its primary branch by the chosen random angle. Then, it is globally scaled right before it is attached to the tree such that the length of its scaled primary branch matches that of the end branch being replaced. Once scaled, the primary branch of the replication block replaces the end-branch. This growth is capped by the silhouettes of the source images to ensure that the reconstructed overall shape is as close as possible to that of the real tree.

**Constrained growth.**    The reconstructed 3D points, by virtue of being visible, are considered to be very close to the branch endpoints. By branch endpoints, we mean the exposed endpoints of the last generation of the branches. These points are thus used to constrain the extents of the branch structure. By comparison, in the approach described in the previous chapter, the 3D points are primarily used to extract the shapes of leaves.

This constrained growth of branches (resulting in $Tree$) is computed by minimizing $\sum_i D(p_i, Tree)$ over all the 3D points $\{p_i | i = 1, ..., n_{3D}\}$, with $n_{3D}$ being the number of 3D points. $D(p, Tree)$ is the smallest distance between a given point $p$ and the branch endpoints of $Tree$. Unfortunately, the space of all possible subtrees with a fixed number of generations to be added to a given tree is exponential. Instead, we solve this optimization in a greedy manner. For each node of the current tree, we define an *influence cone* with its axis along the current branch and an angular extent of 90° side to side. For that node, only the 3D points that fall within its influence cone are considered. This restricts the number of points and set of subtrees considered in the optimization.

Our problem reduces to minimizing $\sum_{p_i \in Cone} D(p_i, Subtree)$ for each subtree, with $Cone$ being the set of points within the influence cone associated with $Subtree$. If $Cone$ is empty, the branches for this node are created using the unconstrained growth procedure described earlier. The order in which subtrees are computed is in the same order of the size of $Cone$, and it is done generation by generation. The number of generations of branches to be added at a time can be controlled. In our implementation, for speed considerations, we add one generation at a time and set a maximum number of 7 generations.

Once the skeleton and thickness distribution have been computed, the branch structure can be converted into a 3D mesh, as shown in Figures 4.6, 4.3, and 4.7. The user has the option to perform the same basic editing functions as described in Section 4.3.1.

## 4.4 POPULATING THE TREE WITH LEAVES

The previous section described how the extracted 3D point cloud is used to reconstruct the branches. Given the branches, one could always just add the leaves directly on the branches using simple guidelines such as making the leaves point away from branches. While this approach would have the advantage of not requiring the use of the source images, the result may deviate significantly from the look of the real tree we wish to model. Instead, we chose to analyze the source images by segmenting and clustering, and we use the results of the analysis to guide the leaf population process.

### 4.4.1 IMAGE SEGMENTATION AND CLUSTERING

Since the leaves appear relatively repetitive, one could conceivably use texture analysis for image segmentation. Unfortunately, the spatially-varying amounts of foreshortening and mutual occlusion of leaves significantly complicate the use of texture analysis. However, we do not require very accurate leaf-by-leaf segmentation to produce models of realistic-looking trees.

We assume that the color for a leaf is homogeneous and there are intensity edges between adjacent leaves. We first apply the mean shift filter (Comaniciu and Meer (2002)) to produce homogeneous regions, with each region tagged with a mean-shift color. These regions undergo a split or merge operation to produce new regions within a prescribed range of sizes. These new regions are then clustered based on the mean-shift colors. Each cluster is a set of new regions with similar color and size that are distributed in space as can be seen in Figure 4.5(c,d). These three steps are detailed below.

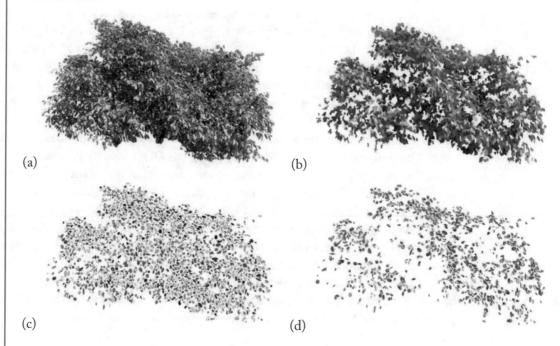

(a)

(b)

(c)

(d)

**Figure 4.5:** Segmentation and clustering. (a) Matted leaves from source image, (b) regions created after the mean shift filtering, (c) the first 30 clusters (color-coded by cluster), and (d) 17 textured clusters (textures from source images).

1. **Mean shift filtering.** The mean shift filter is performed on color and space jointly. We map the RGB color space into LUV space, which is more perceptually meaningful. We define our multivariate kernel as the product of two radially symmetric kernels: $K_{h_s,h_r}(\mathbf{x}) = \frac{C}{h_s^2 h_r^2} k_E\left(\left|\frac{\mathbf{x}_s}{h_s}\right|^2\right) k_E\left(\left|\frac{\mathbf{x}_r}{h_r}\right|^2\right)$, where $\mathbf{x}_s$ is the spatial vector (2D coordinates), $\mathbf{x}_r$ is the color vector in LUV, and $C$ is the normalization constant. $k_E(x)$ the profile of Epanechnikov kernel, $k_E(x) = 1 - x$ if $0 \le x \le 1$, and 0 for $x > 1$. The bandwidth parameters $h_s$ and $h_r$ are interactively set by the user. In our experiments, $h_s$ ranged from 6 to 8 and $h_r$ from 3 to 7. The segmentation results were reasonable as long as the values used were within the specified ranges.

2. **Region split or merge.** After applying mean-shift filtering, we build a graph on the image grid with each pixel as a node; edges are established between 8-neighboring nodes if their (mean-shift) color difference is below a threshold (1 in our implementation). Prior to the split or merge operation, the user specifies the range of valid leaf sizes. Connected regions that are

too small are merged with neighboring ones until a valid size is reached. On the other hand, connected regions that are too large are split into smaller valid ones. Splitting is done by seeding and region growing; the seeds can be either automatic by even distribution or interactively set. This split or merge operation produces a set of new regions.

3. **Color-based clustering.** Each new region is considered a candidate leaf. We use a $K$-means clustering method to obtain about 20 to 30 clusters. We only keep about 10 clusters associated with the brightest colors as they are much more likely to represent visible leaves. Each new region in the kept clusters is fitted to an ellipse through singular value decomposition (SVD).

**User interaction.**   The user can click to add a seed for splitting and creating a new region or click on a specific cluster to accept or reject it. With the exception of the fig tree shown in Figure 4.6, the leaves were fully automatically segmented. (For the fig tree, the user manually specified a few boundary regions and clusters.)

## 4.4.2   ADDING LEAVES TO BRANCHES

There are two types of leaves that are added to the tree model: leaves that are created from the source images using the results of segmentation and clustering (Section 4.4.1), and leaves that are synthesized to fill in areas that either are occluded or lack coverage from the source viewpoints.

**Creating leaves from segmentation.**   Once we have produced the clusters, we now proceed to compute their 3D locations. Recall that each region in a cluster represents a leaf. We also have a user-specified generic leaf model for each tree example (usually an ellipse, but a more complicated model is possible). For each region in each source image, we first find the closest pre-computed 3D point (Section 4.2) or branch (Section 4.3) along the line of sight of the region's centroid. The 3D location of the leaf is then snapped to the closest pre-computed 3D point or nearest 3D position on the branch. Using branches to create leaves is necessary to make up for the possible lack of pre-computed 3D points (say, due to using a small number of source images).

The orientation of the generic leaf model is initially set to be parallel to the source image plane. In the case where more than three pre-computed 3D points project onto a region, SVD is applied to all these points to compute the leaf's orientation. Otherwise, its orientation is such that its projection is closest to the region shape.

This approach of leaf generation is simple and fast and is applied to each of the source images. However, since we do not compute the explicit correspondences of regions in different views, it typically results in multiple leaves for a given corresponding leaf region. (Correspondence is not computed because our automatic segmentation technique does not guarantee consistent segmentation across the source images.) We just use a distance threshold (half the width of a leaf) to remove redundant leaves.

**Synthesizing missing leaves.**   Because of lack of coverage by the source images and occlusion, the tree model that has been reconstructed thus far may be missing a significant number of leaves. To overcome this limitation, we synthesize leaves on the branch structure to produce a more evenly distributed leaf density.

The leaf density on a branch is computed as the ratio of the number of leaves on the branch to the length of the branch. We synthesize leaves on branches with the lowest leaf densities (bottom third) using the branches with the highest leaf densities (top third) as exemplars.

## 4.5   RESULTS

In this section, we show reconstruction results for a variety of trees. The recovered models have leaves numbering from about 3,000 to 140,000. We used Maya$^{TM}$ for rendering; note that we did not model complex phenomena such as inter-reflection and subsurface scattering of leaves. In our experiments, image acquisition using an off-the-shelf digital camera took about 10 minutes. The computation time depends on the complexity of the tree. Automatic visible branch reconstruction took 1-3 minutes while manual editing took about 5 minutes. Invisible branches were reconstructed in about 5 minutes while leaf segmentation took about 1 minute per image. The final stage of leaf population took 3-5 minutes.

The fig tree shown in Figure 4.6 was captured using 18 images covering about 180°. It is a typical but challenging example as there are substantial missing points in the crown. Nevertheless, its shape has been recovered reasonably well, with a plausible-looking branch structure. The process was automatic, with the exceptions of manual addition of a branch and a few adjustments to the thickness of branches.

The potted flower tree shown in Figure 4.7 is an interesting example: the leaf size relative to the entire tree is moderate and not small as in the other examples. Here, 32 source images were taken along a complete 360° path around the tree. Its leaves were discernable enough that our automatic leaf generation technique produced only moderately realistic leaves since larger leaves require more accurate segmentation. The other challenge is the very dense foliage—dense to the extent that only the trunk is clearly visible. In this case, the user supplied only three simple replication blocks shown in Figure 4.4(d); our system then automatically produced a very plausible-looking model. About 60% of the reconstructed leaves relied on the recovered branches for placement. Based on leaf/tree size ratio, this example falls in the middle of the plant/tree spectrum shown in Figure 4.1.

Figure 4.8 shows a medium-sized tree, which was captured with 16 images covering about 135°. The branches took 10 minutes to modify, and the leaf segmentation was fully automatic. The rightmost image in Figure 4.8 shows a view not covered by the source images; here, synthesized leaves are shown as well.

The tree in Figure 4.9 is large with relatively tiny leaves. It was captured with 16 images covering about 120°. We spent five minutes editing the branches after automatic reconstruction to clean up the appearance of the tree. Since the branches are extracted by connecting nearby points,

**Figure 4.6:** Image-based modeling of a fig tree. From left to right: a source image (out of 18 images), reconstructed branch structure rendered at the same viewpoint, tree model rendered at the same viewpoint, and tree model rendered at a different viewpoint.

**Figure 4.7:** Potted flower tree example. (a) One of the source images, (b) reconstructed branches, (c) complete tree model, and (d) model seen from a different viewpoint.

**Figure 4.8:** Medium-sized tree example. From left to right: one of the source images, reconstructed tree model, and model rendered at a different viewpoint.

branches that are close to each other may be merged. The rightmost visible branch in Figure 4.9 is an example of a merged branch.

## 4.6 DISCUSSION

There are certainly ways of improving our system. For one, the replication block need not necessarily be restricted to being part of the visible branches in the same tree. It is possible to generate a much larger and tree-specific database of replication blocks. The observed set of replication blocks can be used to fetch the appropriate database for branch generation, thus providing a richer set of branch shapes.

Our system currently requires that the images be pre-segmented into tree branches, tree leaves, and background. Although there are many automatic techniques for segmentation, the degree of automation for *reliable* segmentation is highly dependent on the complexity of the tree and background. We currently do not see an adequate solution to this issue without adequate hints from the user (see Chapter 5 for another approach).

## 4.7 SUMMARY

We have described a system for constructing realistic-looking tree models from images. Our system was designed with the goal of minimizing user interaction in mind. To this end, we devised automatic techniques for recovering visible branches and for segmenting leaves in the source images. The visible branches form replication blocks, which are then used to hallucinate the occluded branches.

**Figure 4.9:** Large tree example. Two of the source images are shown in (a) and (c), with the reconstructed model rendered at the same viewpoints shown in (b) and (d), respectively. The recovered branches are shown in (e) while a new oblique view of the reconstructed model is shown in (f).

Unfortunately, the leaves are small and tend to look different at different views. So, rather than attempting to recover the 3D location of leaves through stereo on the multiple input images (which is very difficult to do reliably), we instead backproject the 2D leaves in the source images onto the nearest recovered 3D branches. This heuristic is acceptable because the end result is still a visually-plausible tree model.

CHAPTER 5

# Single Image Tree Modeling

The previous two chapters dealt with plant and tree modeling from multiple images. What if only a single view of the tree is available? In this chapter, we describe a technique to address this constraint. Note that we are not handling single images of plants—extracting generic leaves and unstructured branches from single images is extremely challenging.

## 5.1 OVERVIEW OF SYSTEM

To generate the 3D tree model from a single image, the user is required to draw strokes on the image. There are two sets of strokes: one set to indicate the crown region, within which the leaves are located, and another set to indicate the main trunk and secondary branches.

The system uses the pixel information derived from the strokes on branches to extract the boundaries of branches in the image. This is done to reduce user effort. A few other strokes on remaining branches may be required to complete the process. The branch structure patterns encoded in visible branches are used to construct a small library of elementary subtrees to grow the entire tree. If too few visible branches are available, the tree could also be grown according to some predefined subtree patterns (say, from a different image or from a library derived using the technique described in Chapter 4).

Once the branches have been created, leaves can be generated easily based on the branch structure and image information. One example can be seen in Figure 5.1. The input single image is shown in (a), with two strokes drawn by the user in (b). Our system first grows a branch structure illustrated in (c), then completes the tree with leaves as shown in (d).

## 5.2 IMAGE PLANE SKETCHING

Certain image-based methods, such as that described in Chapter 4 and those of Reche-Martinez et al. (2004) and Neubert et al. (2007), require the tree to be first segmented into branch, leaf, and background regions. Unfortunately, high-quality segmentation is typically difficult to achieve without a significant amount of manual input. Our system does not depend on high quality segmentation. Instead, the user need only draw a few strokes to mark out foliage and visible branches. The segmentation is done using the stroke information and priors on tree structure.

**User interface.** The user draws strokes on the image by moving the mouse cursor and holding a button. (Left button for the crown and right button for branches.) A similar UI is designed

(a)

(b)

(c)

(d)

**Figure 5.1:** Single image tree modeling. (a) Single input image of a tree downloaded from www.flickr.com. (b) Strokes drawn by the user, only two strokes for this example. (c) The automatic synthesis of the tree branches. (d) The complete tree model rendered at the same viewpoint as the input image.

by Li et al. (2004) for image segmentation. For simplicity, we always use one stroke to mark the crown. The foliage region is automatically extracted by the method described in the following paragraph according to this stroke. The user then draws strokes to mark out branches. After each branch stroke, a tracing algorithm is triggered to follow the visible branches close to the stroke. The traced visible branches are displayed over the image. If not satisfied with this result, the user has the option of adding or deleting strokes for correction. Unlike a pure sketching system (Okabe et al. (2005)), we have the image information underlying the drawn strokes that allows extremely simple sketching.

Figure 5.1 shows an example in which we need only two strokes: the first crown stroke in red and the second branch stroke in blue.

**Foliage extraction.**    Foliage is extracted from the closed region by the first crown stroke, which roughly follows the crown boundary. 'GrabCut' (Rother et al. (2004)) extracts an object inside a bounding rectangle by analyzing the different appearance inside and outside of the rectangle. The 'GrabCut' approach is less effective here as both inside and outside of the crown stroke could contain a significant number of leaf colors. For extraction, we simply compute a Gaussian mixture model (GMM) for the pixel RGB values in the region closed by the crown stroke. We employ a mixture of 10 Gaussians for large variation of colors due to the background. Then we take the four most green or red Gaussian components as leaf clusters, and the remaining six components are considered as background clusters. With these appearance models $G(I_x, \theta^{\mathcal{F}})$, $G(I_x, \theta^{\mathcal{B}})$ for the foreground and background, we compute a graph-cut based extraction to detect leaf pixels. Here, $G(\cdot, \theta)$ is the pdf function of the GMM distribution, $I_x$ indicates the RGB values at pixel $x$, $\theta^{\mathcal{F}}$, and $\theta^{\mathcal{B}}$ are GMM parameters.

At each pixel $x$, we compute a $0 - 1$ label $\beta_x$ via graph cut, where $\beta_x = 0$ represents leaf pixels and $\beta_x = 1$ represents background pixels. A Gibbs energy of the following form is defined over the enclosed region of crown stroke

$$\sum_x E_d(\beta_x, \theta^{\mathcal{F}}, \theta^{\mathcal{B}}) + \sum_{(x,y) \in \mathbf{N}} E_s(\beta_x, \beta_y),$$

where $\mathbf{N}$ is the set of all 4-neighbor pixel pairs,

$$E_d(\beta_x, \theta^{\mathcal{F}}, \theta^{\mathcal{B}}) = -\beta_x log G(I_x, \theta^{\mathcal{B}}) - (1 - \beta_x) log G(I_x, \theta^{\mathcal{F}})$$

is the data term, and

$$E_s(\beta_x, \beta_y) = \begin{cases} 0 & \beta_x = \beta_y \\ \lambda / |I_x - I_y| & \beta_x \neq \beta_y \end{cases}$$

is the smoothness term. A graph-cut algorithm (Kolmogorov and Zabih (2002)) is applied to minimize this Gibbs energy by assigning a 0 or 1 for each $\beta_x$. The constant $\lambda$, indicating the strength of smoothness, is set to 60 in our implementation. Before the extraction, we usually expand the enclosed region by morphology operations to allow more freedom for the sketching by the user.

**Figure 5.2:** The extracted foliage region via minimizing the Gibbs energy. These are the results for the cherry tree in Figure 5.1 and the oak tree in Figure 5.7. Note that our modeling needs only a coarse segmentation.

Figure 5.2 shows the result of the foliage extraction from the input image and the stroke in Figure 5.1. Note that one important advantage of our system is that it does not require very accurate segmentation.

**Visible branch tracing.**   To reduce the required amount of user interaction, the system automatically traces along branch strokes to detect nearby visible branches in the image. This tracing is trigged after each branch stroke is drawn. We apply a method inspired by the 'Lazy Snapping' method (Li et al. (2004)). Pixels on the branch stroke are used as samples to compute an appearance model for the branch. All the other pixels are samples to compute the non-branch appearance. Again, a GMM model is used for the appearance model. Since the branch stroke could cover leaf pixels (e.g., in the first example in Figure 5.7), we discard the Gaussian component in the branch GMM if it is too close to some component in the foliage GMM $G(I_x, \theta^{\mathcal{F}})$. The branch appearance model is denoted as $G(I_x, \theta^{\mathcal{T}})$. The appearance model for non-branch pixels is $G(I_x, \theta^{\mathcal{N}})$. Typically, 5 Gaussian distributions are used for each model.

With these two appearance models, we move a circle along the branch stroke from bottom to top. At each position, pixels on the circle are classified as branch pixel or non-branch pixel by a maximum likelihood estimation. We use a $0 - 1$ variable $\alpha$ to facilitate this classification where 0 means branch pixel and 1 for others. For each pixel $x$ on the circle, we compute $\alpha_x$ by maximizing the following likelihood

$$(1 - \alpha_x)G(I_x, \theta^{\mathcal{T}}) + \alpha_x G(I_x, \theta^{\mathcal{N}}).$$

Typically, multiple branch pixels will be detected on the circle, with these pixels forming different clusters. We discard a cluster if there are non-branch pixels along the line segment connecting the cluster center and circle center (via the maximum likelihood estimation). The circle center will move to the remaining cluster center to continue tracing. In the case of multiple clusters left on the circle, they are processed in a breadth-first manner. The branch skeleton is detected by connecting all these circle centers during tracing. This skeleton is overlayed in the image. If the user is not satisfied with

(a)          (b)          (c)

**Figure 5.3:** (a) We move a circle along the branch stroke to trace visible branches. The fork is detected and a new green branch is created automatically. (b) The branch is recovered by connecting all circle centers during tracing. (c) The initial branch is simplified to discard redundant joints.

this result, he or she can add more strokes to correct it or delete wrong branches. The skeleton is then simplified by preserving the updated skeleton topology while discarding redundant joints. A joint is deemed to be redundant if it is not located at a fork and the branch direction does not significantly change at that joint (more specifically, if the angular change between the segments immediately before and after the joint is less than 30°). In our implementation, the circle radius is fixed at 50 pixels in all our examples, with the image resolution being about 1500 × 1500.

At the tree root, the branch thickness is also computed by varying the circle radius to find the largest circle whose pixels are all branch pixels. This thickness computation is unreliable at small twigs. We simply set branch radius to 75% of its parent although better botanical rules can be used according to Weber and Penn (1995).

As shown in Figure 5.3(a), the branch segment indicated by the green line is correctly detected although the drawn stroke does not pass through it. A branch system is retrieved by connecting circle centers in sequence as shown in (b). This initial result contains many fragment line segments, which is undesirable for the non-parametric synthesis in Section 5.3.1. The final branch (after redundant joints were discarded) is shown in (c).

## 5.3    TREE GROWING

Once branches have been recovered, leaves can be generated along them to complete the tree. Many previous tree modeling methods (such as Neubert et al. (2007); Xu et al. (2007) and including the system described in Chapter 4) model trees this way by focusing on the modeling of branch systems.

Once visible branches and the foliage region are extracted from the image, we develop a tree grow engine to automatically generate the whole tree branch in 3D space by following the given image. We only seek a plausible solution that is possible with the tree priors and the inherent self-similar structural patterns of the tree. A production engine similar to that of Xu et al. (2007) and the system described in Chapter 4 is used where 3D points are used to guide the growth.

### 5.3.1   GROWTH ENGINE

The engine starts with the creation of a library of elementary subtrees from the visible branches. Then, a non-parametric synthesis approach is used to systematically generate branches that were occluded in the image.

**Initialization.**   There are two parts in the initialization process, namely conversion of 2D branches (from the image) to 3D and generation of the subtree library.

- **Conversion of 2D branches into 3D:** Visible branches interactively traced in Section 5.2 are defined in the image plane. We first convert these branches from 2D to 3D before growing. From a single image, there is not enough information to accurately reconstruct the branch position in 3D space. Here, we employ the approach proposed in Okabe et al. (2005) to generate a 3D branch structure from the extracted visible branches. The basic idea is to distribute branches in 3D space evenly and keep their image projections unchanged. Here, we assume an orthographic camera model to relate 3D branch position and image coordinate.

- **Creation of the library:** We then built a library of elementary subtrees. These library subtrees are built from the recovered visible branches by taking all its subtrees. If there are too few subtrees (as in the first example in Figure 5.7), we add predefined subtrees in the library. Figure 5.4 shows the predefined subtrees in our implemented system. Obviously, this predefined library can be further enriched to handle larger varieties of trees. It is remarkable that we produced all of our results with only at most 8 subtrees in the current implementation.

**Non-parametric synthesis.**   Starting from the 3D visible branch and a library, we take a non-parametric approach to grow a tree. The synthesis process simply iteratively replaces an existing branch by a library subtree. Figure 5.4 shows a single step of the non-parametric branch growth. There are two types of branch replacement in our system. In type I replacement, new branches grow at the end of its 'supporting branch' (i.e., shown as the red segment in a subtree). In type II replacement, new branches can grow along the 'supporting branch.'

The selection of the branch to be replaced and the library subtree is driven by minimizing the cost function defined in Section 5.3.2. Each time, the resulting synthesis is pruned by the extracted foliage silhouette. Usually, we run the following three steps iteratively about 100 times for each tree:

- **Selection of a branch to be replaced:** We go through a small set of existing branches and take the one whose replacement gives the lowest cost function defined in Section 5.3.2.

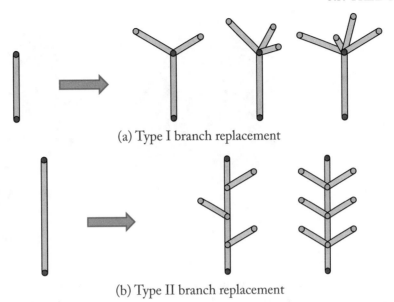

(a) Type I branch replacement

(b) Type II branch replacement

**Figure 5.4:** A branch is replaced by a library subtree. We call the red branch in the subtree as 'supporting branch' for ease of reference.

To create this set of existing branches, we choose branches with larger radius and older generation. We sort all existing branches according to their radius. Then branches are selected sequentially from the sorted array. Each branch is selected with a probability, which is inversely proportional to its generation.

- **Selection of a replacing library subtree:** For the selected branch to be replaced, we search all the available library subtrees (at most (8) to find that one giving the lowest cost of the function defined in Section 5.3.2.

Except for the subtrees generated from visible branches, the user can add predefined subtrees: type I, type II or both. A subtree is rotated around its 'supporting branch' and scaled before it is used to replace some existing branch. There are two parameters to be determined in this operation.

  - The rotation angle of the subtree around its 'supporting branch' is searched among 12 quantized levels of 360 degrees that gives the lowest cost.
  - The scaling factor of the subtree is determined such that its 'supporting branch' is of the same length as the replaced branch.

- **Branch pruning:** After replacement, the resulting branches are pruned based on the detected foliage region and the existing branches. Any branch going beyond the foliage region is removed, as are the new branches if they are too close to some existing branches.

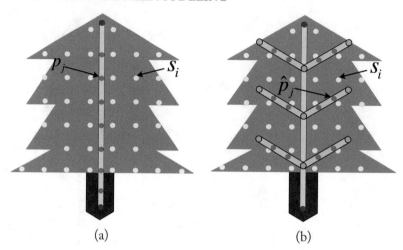

**Figure 5.5:** Yellow points in the foliage region are the image attractors. (a) Blue points are sampled over the tree to compute the distance between an attractor and the tree. (b) After branch replacement, the distance between attractors and the tree is updated according to newly created branches.

### 5.3.2   DATA-DRIVEN ATTRACTORS

The growth engine is driven by the data to produce a realistic result. The input image information is 2D and only weakly controls the growth in the desired tree volume. Hence, we introduce some 3D points based on heuristics to control the growth better.

**Image attractors.**   To make the result after growing similar to the image, we define a set of image attractors $s_i, i = \{1, 2, \cdots N\}$ that are sampled evenly in the foliage region with a fixed interval as illustrated by the yellow points in Figure 5.5 (a). These attractors control the tree growth by requiring that each attractor should be close to the resulting tree $T$. The growth is then driven by minimizing a cost defined as $E^{2D}(T) = \sum_i dist(s_i, T)$, where $dist(s_i, T)$ is the distance of an attractor $s_i$ to the projection of tree $T$ onto the image. To compute $dist(s_i, T)$, we also sample a set of points $p_i, i = \{1, 2, \cdots M\}$ along the image projection of the tree $T$ as the blue points in Figure 5.5 (a). The distance function is then defined as $dist(s_i, T) = \min_j(dist(s_i, p_j))$.

**Extrapolated 3D attractors.**   The image driven growth could lead to an unbalanced tree, where only front branches are generated. This is because such an unbalanced tree can minimize the cost $E^{2D}(T)$ well without any back branches. Similar problems exist in previous sketching systems such as Okabe et al. (2005). To alleviate this problem, the tree is rotated 90 degrees around its main trunk and merged with the original one, as in Okabe et al. (2005). This method solves the problem at the cost of creating inconsistent visible branches with the image.

We introduce some extrapolated 3D points to balance the tree growth. We rotate the existing tree by $90°$, but only keep its branch joints $d_i, i = \{1, 2, \cdots K\}$. These joints are used as 3D space attractors to drive branch replacement in a similar manner to image attractors. Here the distance between these 3D points and the tree is to be minimized and the cost is defined as $E^{3D}(T) = \sum_i dist(d_i, T)$. $dist(d_i, T)$ is the distance between the 3D point $d_i$ and the tree $T$. Again, the tree $T$ is sampled as a set of points $t_i, i = \{1, 2, \cdots, L\}$ in 3D space along the branch skeleton to compute the $dist(d_i, T) = \min_j(dist(d_i, t_j))$.

In our current implementation, the growth is driven by alternating the image attractors and the 3D point attractors. Figure 5.6 illustrates the effectiveness of this alternating strategy. The pure image driven growth yields good results when viewed from the same direction as the input image, as in (a), and unnatural results (b) viewed from an orthogonal viewpoint. By alternating the image driven growth and 3D point driven growth, a better result can be obtained in (c) and (d).

**Speedup.**    The growth engine involves a large amount of computation of the distances between the attractors and the tree. In each replacement iteration, we only add more branches to the tree and no existing branch is discarded. So the distance computation in the previous iteration can be reused for speedup purposes. For each attractor $s$ (no matter image point or 3D point), we record its distance to the tree $T^n$ at the $n$−th iteration as $d_s^n$. At the $n + 1$−th iteration, we compute the distance between $s$ and newly created branches as $\hat{d}_s$. The distance between $s$ and $T^{n+1}$ is then updated as $d_s^{n+1} = min\{d_s^n, \hat{d}_s\}$. This is illustrated in Figure 5.5(b).

## 5.4    COMPLETING THE TREE

The leaves of the tree are automatically synthesized from the recovered branch structure and textured with the input image. Each leaf is represented by a flat rectangle with the size of 1/10 of the main trunk radius. Each branch generates from a range of 50 to 200 leaves proportional to it length. The arrangement of the leaves around the branch is randomized. We keep only those leaves that are projected inside the foliage region in the input image. Leaves are textured according to their projected position on the input image. The generic leaf shape, leaf size, density and arrangement of leaves along a branch are all parameterized in our current implementation. But the default values are used throughout all examples of this chapter.

## 5.5    RESULTS

We tested our system on several different examples to demonstrate its effectiveness. One example (image of a cherry tree downloaded from www.flickr.com) is shown in Figure 5.1. Its foliage region is shown in Figure 5.2, and its branch tracing procedure is illustrated in Figure 5.3. The complete branching structure generated by the growth engine is shown in Figure 5.1(c). A rendering of the final cherry tree model is shown in Figure 5.1(d). For this example, we drew two strokes and used both subtrees of visible branches and predefined subtrees of type I. Branch tracing was performed

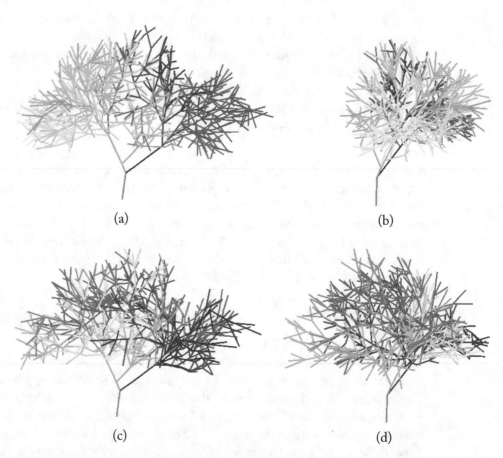

(a)

(b)

(c)

(d)

**Figure 5.6:** (a) and (b) are the branches generated by image driven growth viewed from the front and side. Although the image driven growth can guarantee the result similar to the image in front, the result looks unnatural from the side. (c) and (d) are results computed by alternating image driven growth and 3D point driven growth. Both front and side results look good.

(a)                    (b)                    (c)                    (d)

**Figure 5.7:** Examples are sorted by increasing number of strokes: (a) The single input image. (b) The synthesized branch structure. (c) Complete tree model with leaves rendered at the same viewpoint as the input image. (d) Rendered from a novel view point.

**Figure 5.8:** Modeling woods with multiple trees. On the top is the input image. The rendering of the recovered model is at the bottom.

**Figure 5.9:** Street-side tree modeling: several input images captured along a street in the top row, and the tree models rendered at the same viewpoint on the bottom row.

in real-time, which provides instant feedback to the user to decide if additional branch strokes are needed. In our implementation, the growing of branches typically took about 20 minutes on a PC with 2.4GHz CPU. The population of the tree with leaves took another 10 minutes.

More examples are shown in Figure 5.7. For the sycamore tree in the first row, only two strokes were used. The tracing did not add any more branches. Its branching structure was entirely synthesized from the library of predefined subtrees of type II. For the oak tree in the second row, three strokes were drawn. Part of its visible branches were traced automatically, but one is missing due to the dense foliage and was added using a second branch stroke. For the second cherry tree, it took 3 strokes for the branches as the tracing was more challenging. The oak tree and cherry tree were both downloaded from www.flickr.com.

The simplicity of our method made modeling tractable even for a single image that contains multiple trees. Given the image shown in Figure 5.8, we are able to extract four tree models using only 16 strokes on the input image. (The relative positions of trees in 3D were manually set.) A more systematic usage of our system in urban environments is shown in Figure 5.9. Trees along a street can only be captured from close viewpoints due to space constraints, which makes previous image-based tree modeling methods less applicable. Here, we modeled each tree from a single image, then aligned all trees manually in 3D. In Figure 5.9, the seven trees were modeled with 2, 2, 5, 3, 3, 2, and 2 strokes, respectively, from left to right. All trees were grown with predefined subtrees of type I.

## 5.6   SUMMARY

We have described a simple and effective system for constructing realistic tree models from a single image. Our system was designed to minimize user interaction. The resulting system is simple and practical in that a user with little experience need only sketch a few strokes on the single input image.

The system can be improved or extended in different ways. For example, it would be interesting to see if large databases of images where trees have been pre-segmented can, through learning, be used to further reduce the requirement for strokes and increase the accuracy of segmentation. The use of a more extensive tree library containing tree growth parameters and global tree shapes (along the lines of Chen et al. (2008)) may help generate even more plausible-looking models. Finally, there is room for speeding up the branch growth and leaf completion processes, which would further enhance the modeling experience.

CHAPTER 6

# Summary and Concluding Remarks

We have described three image-based techniques to generate 3D models of plants or trees from images. The techniques need to be customized based on the assumptions on the complexity of the plant or tree and the number of images used for modeling.

Chapter 3 shows how we can generate models of plants from multiple images; here, all the visible leaves are modeled using the extracted 3D point cloud while branches are interactively created through a 2D-3D interface. The branches have to be produced in this manner because of the significant occlusions in the images and botanical rules are much harder to apply.

Trees with relatively small leaves cannot be easily modeled using the technique described in Chapter 3. On the other hand, trees are more easily characterized using botany rules. As described in Chapter 4, the technique is modified to recover the shape of the trunk and branches in order to extract what we call "replication blocks", the simplest of which is a Y-structure consisting of a parent branch and at least two immediate child branches. They are used to hallucinate the structure hidden by the leaves. The 3D location and shapes of the leaves cannot simply be extracted applying stereo on the input images because of occlusion and because the appearance of leaves can change drastically over the different views. Instead, we backproject 2D leaves onto the closest reconstructed 3D branches.

What if we have only a single image of a tree or trees? Chapter 5 shows how tree modeling can be done, albeit with more user interaction. The user needs to indicate where the foliage is and where representative branches are. The sampled data are used for the appropriate segmentation of leaves and branches, after which a branch growth algorithm similar to that in Chapter 4 is applied. Because only one view is available, the growth needs an additional prior; in this case, the branches have to be well-distributed in space.

What have we learnt? Image-based techniques have to be customized in order to work well. Occlusions and appearance changes with viewpoint are the perennial problems associated with image-based techniques, and priors on the shape of the plant or tree are absolutely necessary to produce visually-plausible models. Computer vision techniques are never foolproof, which necessitates some form of user interaction for correction.

Image-based techniques, when designed well, can produce models that are close to reality and thus are visually plausible. There is, of course, a major downside—we can only model what exists. However, having models of real trees can help in generation of new trees. For example, one can "reverse-engineer" the growth parameters of real trees and learn the span of parameter space of real trees, which can be used to create new visually-plausible trees and possibly predict their appearance. (Note that the "reverse-engineer" process is highly non-trivial and is an interesting topic of investigation.) New trees may also be generated by "cutting-and-pasting" subtrees, though this operation may need to be done with care.

Is complete automation possible? Is complete automation always desirable? Our answer to both: probably not. As we said earlier, computer vision techniques are not perfect, and manual corrections or hints will be necessary. While what is visible is immutable (unless one wishes to change the laws of geometry), there is some degree of freedom in specifying the shape of branches or leaves that are occluded. This is where the user should be given a fair amount of control, e.g., on the density of branches and leaves. The amount of control will depend on the requirements associated with model generation.

Ultimately, the ideal technique depends on the relative importance of a number of factors: ease of use (related to complexity of system), flexibility, visual plausibility, and accuracy expected. Image-based techniques may be an overkill if only cartoon-like trees are required for construction of an environment for non-photorealistic games. However, we expect that realism is expected in many scenarios, not just games, but in the movie industry, to enable scientific study of plants, for web-based applications that feature 3D terrain maps (such as Google Earth and Virtual Earth), as well as for architectural visualization. We hope that our book will serve as a guide to understand some of the issues for plant and tree modeling. We also hope that our image-based techniques will be good starting points for anyone wishing to design a tree or plant modeling system.

# CHAPTER 7

# Acknowledgments

This book is based on our SIGGRAPH publications on modeling plants (Quan et al. (2006)) and trees (Tan et al. (2007)), and SIGGRAPH Asia publication on single image tree modeling (Tan et al. (2008)). We would like to thank our co-authors of those papers, namely, Ping Tan, Gang Zeng, Jingdong Wang, Lu Yuan, Tian Fang, Jianxiong Xiao, and Peng Zhao.

We would also like to thank Oscar Au and Tian Fang for their assistance in rendering some of the results seen in this book. Long Quan would like to acknowledge the support by Hong Kong RGC Grant 619107 and 618908.

Finally, we are grateful to the various authors and publishers for giving us permission to use their figures in our review chapter (Chapter 2).

# Bibliography

H. Abelson and A. diSessa, *Turtle Geometry*, MIT Press, Cambridge, 1982.

P. Besl and N. McKay, "A method for registration of 3D shapes," *IEEE Transactions on Pattern Analysis and Machine Intelligence*, 14(2):239–256, 1992. DOI: 10.1109/34.121791

F. Boudon, P. Prusinkiewicz, P. Federl, C. Godin, and R. Karwowski, "Interactive design of bonsai tree models," *Eurographics, Computer Graphics Forum*, 22(3):591–599, 2003. DOI: 10.1111/1467-8659.t01-2-00707

K. Boulanger, S. Pattanaik, and K. Bouatouch, "Rendering grass terrains in real-time with dynamic lighting," *ACM SIGGRAPH Sketches*, 2006. DOI: 10.1145/1179849.1179907

Y. Boykov, O. Veksler, and R. Zabih, "Fast approximate energy minimization via graph cuts," *IEEE Transactions on Pattern Analysis and Machine Intelligence*, 23(11):1222–1239, 2001. DOI: 10.1109/34.969114

S. Brasch, E.G. McPherson, and L. Linsen, "Visualization of time-varying natural tree data," *IASTED International Conference on Visualization, Imaging, and Image Processing (VIIP)*, 2007.

T.P. Breckon and R.B. Fisher, "Non-parametric 3D surface completion," *Int'l Conf. on 3-D Digital Imaging and Modeling*, pp. 573–580, 2005. DOI: 10.1109/3DIM.2005.61

G.J. Brostow, I. Essa, D. Steedly, and V. Kwatra, "Novel skeletal representation for articulated creatures," *European Conference on Computer Vision*, pp. 66–78, 2004.

X. Chen, B. Neubert, Y.-Q. Xu, O. Deussen, and S.B. Kang, "Sketch-based tree modeling using Markov random field," *ACM SIGGRAPH Asia and ACM Transaction on Graphics*, 27(5), article 109, 2008. DOI: 10.1145/1409060.1409062

N. Chiba, S. Ohkawa, K. Muraoka, and M. Miura, "Visual simulation of botanical trees based on virtual heliotropism and dormancy break," *Journal of Visualization and Computer Animation*, vol. 5, pp. 3–-15, 1994. DOI: 10.1002/vis.4340050102

D. Comaniciu and P. Meer, "Mean shift: A robust approach toward feature space analysis," *IEEE Transactions on Pattern Analysis and Machine Intelligence*, 24(5):603–619, 2002. DOI: 10.1109/34.1000236

P. de Reffye, C. Edelin, J. Francon, M. Jaeger, and C. Puech, "Plant models faithful to botanical structure and development," *SIGGRAPH*, pp. 151–158, 1988. DOI: 10.1145/378456.378505

B. Desbenoit, D. Vanderhaghe, E. Galin and J. Grosjean, "Interactive modeling of mushrooms," *Eurographics*, 23(3):37-40, 2004.

B. Desbenoit, E. Galin and S. Akkouche, "Simulating and modeling lichen growth," *Eurographics*, 23(3):341-350, 2004.

O. Deussen and B. Lintermann, *Digital Design of Nature - Computer Generated Plants and Organics*, Springer-Verlag, 2005.

A.A. Efros and T.K. Leung, "Texture synthesis by non-parametric sampling," *IEEE International Conference on Computer Vision*, pp. 1033--1038, 1999. DOI: 10.1109/ICCV.1999.790383

O. Faugeras, Q. Luong, and T. Papadopoulo, *The Geometry of Multiple Images*, The MIT Press, Cambridge, MA, 2001.

M. Goesele, N. Snavely, B. Curless, H. Hoppe, and S.M. Seitz, "Multi-view stereo for community photo collections," *International Conference on Computer Vision*, 2007. DOI: 10.1109/ICCV.2007.4408933

N. Greene, "Voxel space automata: Modeling with stochastic growth processes in voxel space," *ACM SIGGRAPH*, 23(4):175--184, 1989. DOI: 10.1145/74333.74351

F. Han and S.-C. Zhu, "Bayesian reconstruction of 3D shapes and scenes from a single image," *IEEE Workshop on Higher-Level Knowledge in 3D Modeling and Motion Analysis*, pp. 12–20, 2003.

J.S. Hanan, *Parametric L-systems and Their Application to the Modelling and Visualization of Plants*. PhD thesis, University of Regina, June 1992.

J. Hart and B. Baker, "Implicit modeling of tree surfaces," *Implicit Surfaces*, pp. 143–152, 1996.

R. Hartley and A. Zisserman, *Multiple View Geometry in Computer Vision*, Cambridge University Press, 2000.

M. Holton, "Strands, gravity and botanical tree imagery," *Computer Graphics Forum*, 13(1):57–67, 1994. DOI: 10.1111/1467-8659.1310057

H. Honda, P.B. Tomlinson, and J.B. Fisher, "Computer simulation of branch interaction and regulation by unequal flow rates in botanical trees," *American Journal of Botany*, vol. 68, pp. 569--585, 1981.

T. Ijiri, M. Okabe, S. Owada, and T. Igarashi, "Floral diagrams and inflorescences: Interactive flower modeling using botanical structural constraints," *ACM SIGGRAPH and ACM Transactions on Graphics*, 24(3):720–726, 2005. DOI: 10.1145/1185657.1185780

T. Ijiri, S. Owada, and T. Igarashi, "The Sketch L-System: Global control of tree modeling using free-form strokes," *Smart Graphics*, pp. 138–146, 2006. DOI: 10.1007/11795018_13

T. Ijiri, M. Yokoo, S. Kawabata, and T. Igarashi, "Surface-based growth simulation for opening flowers," *Graphics Interface*, pp. 227–234, 2008.

N. Kanamaru, N. Chiba, K. Takahashi, and N. Saito, "CG simulation of natural shapes of botanical trees based on heliotropism," *Transactions of the Institute of Electronics, Information, and Communication Engineers (J75-D-II)*, vol. 1, pp. 76--85, 1992 (in Japanese).

V. Kolmogorov and R. Zabih, "What energy functions can be minimized via graph cuts?," *European Conference on Computer Vision*, vol. III, pp. 65–81, 2002. DOI: 10.1109/TPAMI.2004.1262177

S. Lefebvre and F. Neyret, "Synthesizing bark," *Eurographics Workshop on Rendering*, pp. 105–116, 2002.

M. Lhuillier and L. Quan, "A quasi-dense approach to surface reconstruction from uncalibrated images," *IEEE Transactions on Pattern Analysis and Machine Intelligence*, 27(3):418–433, 2005. DOI: 10.1109/TPAMI.2005.44

Y. Li, J. Sun, C.-K. Tang, and H.-Y. Shum, "Lazy snapping," *ACM SIGGRAPH and ACM Transactions on Graphics*, 23(3):303–308, 2004. DOI: 10.1145/1186562.1015719

C.M. Liddell and D. Hansen, "Visualizing complex biological interactions in the soil ecosystem," *The Journal of Visualization and Computer Animation*, vol. 4, pp. 3--12, 1993. DOI: 10.1002/vis.4340040103

A. Lindenmayer, "Mathematical models for cellular interaction in development, Parts I and II," *Journal of Theoretical Biology*, vol. 18, pp. 280–315, 1968. DOI: 10.1016/0022-5193(68)90079-9

B. Lintermann and O. Deussen, "Interactive modeling of plants," *IEEE Computer Graphics and Applications*, 19(1):56–65, 1999. DOI: 10.1109/38.736469

C. Linz, A. Reche, G. Drettakis, and M. Magnor, "Effective multi-resolution rendering and texture compression for captured volumetric trees," *Eurographics Workshop on Natural Phenomena*, 2006.

R. Mech and P. Prusinkiewicz, "Visual models of plants interacting with their environment," *ACM SIGGRAPH*, pp. 397–410, 1996. DOI: 10.1145/237170.237279

B. Neubert, T. Franken, and O. Deussen, "Approximate image-based tree-modelling using particle flows," *ACM SIGGRAPH and ACM Transactions on Graphics*, 26(3), article 88, 2007. DOI: 10.1145/1275808.1276487

H. Noser and D. Thalmann, "Simulating life of virtual plants, fishes and butterflies," *Artificial Life and Virtual Reality*, N. Magnenat-Thalmann and D. Thalmann (Eds.), John Wiley and Sons, Ltd, 1994.

H. Noser, S. Rudolph, and P. Stucki, "Physics-enhanced L-systems," *International Conference in Central Europe on Computer Graphics, Visualization and Computer Vision*, vol. 2, pp. 214–221, 2001.

M. Okabe, S. Owada, and T. Igarashi, "Interactive design of botanical trees using freehand sketches and example-based editing," *Computer Graphics Forum (Eurographics)*, 24(3), 2005. DOI: 10.1145/1185657.1185779

K. Onishi, S. Hasuike, Y. Kitamura, and F. Kishino, "Interactive modeling of trees by using growth simulation," *ACM Symposium on Virtual Reality Software and Technology*, pp. 66–72, 2003. DOI: 10.1145/1008653.1008667

P. Oppenheimer, "Real time design and animation of fractal plants and trees," *ACM SIGGRAPH*, vol. 20, pp. 55–64, 1986. DOI: 10.1145/15886.15892

W. Palubicki, K. Horel, S. Longay, A. Runions, B. Lane, R. Mech, and P. Prusinkiewicz, "Self-organizing tree models for image synthesis," *ACM SIGGRAPH and Transactions on Graphics*, 28(3), article 58, 2009. DOI: 10.1145/1576246.1531364

F. Perbet and M.-P. Cani, "Animating prairies in real-time," *Symposium on Interactive 3D Graphics*, pp. 103-110, 2001. DOI: 10.1145/364338.364375

J.L. Power, A.J. Bernheim Brush, P. Prusinkiewicz, and D.H. Salesin, "Interactive arrangement of botanical L-system models," *Symposium on Interactive 3D Graphics*, pp. 175-182, 1999. DOI: 10.1145/300523.300548

P. Prusinkiewicz, "Graphical applications of L-systems," *Graphics Interface*, pp. 247-253, 1986.

P. Prusinkiewicz and A. Lindenmayer, *The Algorithmic Beauty of Plants*, Springer-Verlag, 1990.

P. Prusinkiewicz, M. James, and R. Mech, "Synthetic topiary," *SIGGRAPH*, pp. 351–358, 1994. DOI: 10.1145/192161.192254

P. Prusinkiewicz, M. Hammel, J. Hanan, and R. Mech, "L-systems: From the theory to visual models of plants," *2nd CSIRO Symposium on Computational Challanges in Life Sciences*, M.T. Michalewicz (Ed.), 1996.

P. Prusinkiewicz, L. Muendermann, R. Karwowski, and B. Lane, "The use of positional information in the modeling of plants," *SIGGRAPH*, pp. 289–300, 2001. DOI: 10.1145/383259.383291

L. Quan, P. Tan, G. Zeng, L. Yuan, J. Wang, and S.B. Kang, "Image-based plant modeling," *ACM SIGGRAPH and ACM Transactions on Graphics*, 25(3):772-778, 2006. DOI: 10.1145/1141911.1141929

L. Quan, J. Wang, P. Tan, and L. Yuan, "Image-based modeling by joint segmentation," *International Journal of Computer Vision*, 75(1):135-150, 2007. DOI: 10.1007/s11263-007-0044-1

A. Reche-Martinez, I. Martin, and G. Drettakis, "Volumetric reconstruction and interactive rendering of trees from photographs," *ACM SIGGRAPH and ACM Transactions on Graphics*, 23(3):720–727, 2004. DOI: 10.1145/1186562.1015785

C. Rother, V. Kolmogorov, and A. Blake, "GrabCut: interactive foreground extraction using iterated graph cuts," *ACM SIGGRAPH and ACM Transactions on Graphics*, 23(3):309–314, 2004. DOI: 10.1145/1186562.1015720

S. Rudnick, L. Linsen, and E.G. Mcpherson, "Inverse modeling and animation of growing single-stemmed trees at interactive rates," *International Conference in Central Europe on Computer Graphics, Visualization and Computer Vision*, 2007.

A. Runions, M. Fuhrer, B. Lane, P. Federl, A.-G. Rolland-Lagan, and P. Prusinkiewicz, "Modeling and visualization of leaf venation patterns," *ACM SIGGRAPH and ACM Transactions on Graphics*, 24(3):702–711, 2005.

T. Sakaguchi and J. Ohya, "Modeling and animation of botanical trees for interactive virtual environments," *ACM Symposium on Virtual Reality Software and Technology*, pp. 139–146, 1999. DOI: 10.1145/323663.323685

T. Sakaguchi, "Botanical tree structure modeling based on real image set," *SIGGRAPH Technical Sketch*, p. 272, 1998. DOI: 10.1145/280953.282241

J. Shi and J. Malik, "Normalized cuts and image segmentation," *IEEE Transactions on Pattern Analysis and Machine Intelligence* 22(8):888–905, 2000. DOI: 10.1109/34.868688

I. Shlyakhter, M. Rozenoer, J. Dorsey, and S. Teller, "Reconstructing 3D tree models from instrumented photographs," *IEEE Computer Graphics and Applications*, 21(3):53–61, 2001. DOI: 10.1109/38.920627

R.W. Sumner, *Pattern formation in lichen*, Ph.D. thesis, Department of Electrical Engineering and Computer Science, Massachusetts Institute of Technology, 2001.

P. Tan, G. Zeng, J. Wang, S.B. Kang, and L. Quan, "Image-based tree modeling," *ACM SIGGRAPH and ACM Transactions on Graphics*, 26(3), article 87, 2007. DOI: 10.1145/1275808.1276486

P. Tan, T. Fang, J. Xiao, P. Zhao, and L. Quan, "Single image tree modeling," *ACM SIGGRAPH Asia and ACM Transaction on Graphics*, 27(5), article 108, 2008. DOI: 10.1145/1409060.1409061

A. Takenaka, "A simulation model of tree architecture development based on growth response to local light environment," *Journal of Plant Research*, vol. 107, pp. 321--330, 1994. DOI: 10.1007/BF02344260

E. Tola, V. Lepetit, and P. Fua, "A fast local descriptor for dense matching," *IEEE Conference on Computer Vision and Pattern Recognition*, 2008. DOI: 10.1109/CVPR.2008.4587673

S. Ulam, "Pattern of growth of figures: Mathematical aspects," *Module, Proportion, Symmetry, Rhythm,* G. Keps (ed.), pp. 64–74, 1966.

W. Van Haevre and P. Bekaert, "A simple but effective algorithm to model the competition of virtual plants for light and space," *International Conference in Central Europe on Computer Graphics, Visualization and Computer Vision (WSCG),* 2003.

X. Wang, L. Wang, L. Liu, S. Hu, and B. Guo, "Interactive modeling of tree bark," *Pacific Conference on Computer Graphics and Applications,* 2003.

L. Wang, W. Wang, J. Dorsey, X. Yang, B. Guo, and H.-Y. Shum, "Real-time rendering of plant leaves," *ACM SIGGRAPH and ACM Transactions on Graphics,* 24(3):712–719, 2005. DOI: 10.1145/1186822.1073252

J. Weber and J. Penn, "Creation and rendering of realistic trees," *SIGGRAPH,* pp. 119–127, 1995. DOI: 10.1145/218380.218427

J. Wither, F. Boudon, M.-P. Cani, and C. Godin, "Structure from silhouettes: a new paradigm for fast sketch-based design of trees," *Eurographics, Computer Graphics Forum,* 28(2):541–-550, 2009. DOI: 10.1111/j.1467-8659.2009.01394.x

H. Xu, N. Gossett, and B. Chen, "Knowledge and heuristic-based modeling of laser-scanned trees," *ACM Transactions on Graphics,* 26(4), article 19, 2007. DOI: 10.1145/1289603.1289610

# Authors' Biographies

## SING BING KANG

**Sing Bing Kang** received his Ph.D. in robotics from Carnegie Mellon University, Pittsburgh in 1994. He is Principal Researcher at Microsoft Corporation and adjunct faculty member of the School of Interactive Computing at Georgia Tech. His interests are image-based modeling as well as image and video enhancement. Sing Bing has co-edited two books in computer vision ("Panoramic Vision" and "Emerging Topics in Computer Vision"), and coauthored a book on image-based rendering. He has served as area chair and member of technical committee for the three major computer vision conferences, namely International Conference on Computer Vision (ICCV), IEEE Conference on Computer Vision and Pattern Recognition (CVPR), and European Conference on Computer Vision (ECCV). He was program co-chair for CVPR 2009, and has served as papers committee member for SIGGRAPH 2007, SIGGRAPH Asia 2008, and SIGGRAPH 2009. Sing Bing is currently an Associate Editor for IEEE TPAMI and Associate Editor-in-Chief for IPSJ Transactions on Computer Vision and Applications.

## LONG QUAN

**Long Quan** is a Professor of the Department of Computer Science and Engineering at the Hong Kong University of Science and Technology. He received his Ph.D. in Computer Science from INPL, France, in 1989. Before moving back to Hong Kong in 2001, he has been a French CNRS senior research scientist at INRIA in Grenoble. His research interests are focused on 3D reconstruction, structure from motion, vision geometry, and image-based modeling.

He has served as an Associate Editor of PAMI (IEEE Transactions on Pattern Analysis and Machine Intelligence) and as a Regional Editor of IVC (Image and Vision Computing Journal). He is currently on the editorial board of IJCV (the International Journal of Computer Vision), ELCVIA (the Electronic Letters on Computer Vision and Image Analysis), MVA (Machine Vision and Applications) and Foundations and Trends in Computer Graphics and Vision.

He has served as area chair for ICCV (International Conference on Computer Vision), ECCV (European Conference on Computer Vision), and CVPR (IEEE Computer Vision and Pattern Recognition) and ICPR (IAPR International Conference on Pattern Recognition). He was a Program Chair of ICPR 2006 Computer Vision and Image Analysis, and is a General Chair of ICCV 2011 in Barcelona.

Printed in the United States
by Baker & Taylor Publisher Services